A
FASHION
PARADE

A FASHION PARADE

THE SEEBERGER COLLECTION

PRESENTED BY CELESTINE DARS

BLOND & BRIGGS · LONDON

We wish to thank the publishers of the
following publications, for whom some of these
pictures were originally taken: Editions
Ringier, Femme Chic, Collections, Officiel de
la Couture, La Donna, Noir et Blanc, Adam,
Editions Louchel.

First published 1979 by Blond & Briggs Ltd
London, and Tiptree, Colchester, Essex
© Copyright 1979 text by Celestine Dars
© Copyright 1979 illustrations by Seeberger

SBN 85634 061 8

Printed in Great Britain by litho at
The Anchor Press Ltd and bound by
Wm Brendon & Son Ltd, both of
Tiptree, Essex

THE SEEBERGER COLLECTION

I was in Paris, working on another book, when I first met the Seebergers. Their studio lay in the peace of a small garden in a residential area where comfortable bourgeois stone buildings and pseudo-Renaissance private residences had been built at the turn of the century.

I was received with great courtesy by Jean Seeberger, who insisted, as he had already done on the telephone, that their collection might only be of little interest to me. Such emphatic modesty was almost discouraging. Later, I was to discover how tremendously they valued their unique archives, which represented the work not only of their lifetime, but of their parents too.

I was led into a large room, where Jean, still apologising, produced box after box of prints, all carefully filed in chronological order. I fell in love with them straight away. The pictures were exceptional, with a quality I still find difficult to describe, even now that I am more familiar with them.

I think this distinctive quality springs from the photographers' candour. They never interfered with their subjects, but let the lens record exactly what it saw: a sophisticated and wealthy society able to afford the best designers as well as the most exclusive clothes. The photographs, though taken with great care, were not meant to be works of art. They recorded not only the evolution of fashion but of European society with such faithful description that I immediately wanted to write a book. This book does not pretend to be a history of fashion. Its aim is to place the pictures in their historical context – to relate the select minority shown in the photographs to other social classes and to the turmoils which have shaken the twentieth century. War, social unrest and technological development – the birth of television, for example – are recorded, together with the rise and fall of the hemline.

Couturiers, endowed with flair, talent and sensitivity, perceive changes of atmosphere more acutely than most people. Their creations are prophetic, since they are based on unconscious aspirations. Both Poiret and Dior illustrated this point. Immediately after the Second World War, Dior designed a smooth and extremely feminine collection every garment of which required huge amounts of fabric at a time when all materials were in short supply. Women had barely emerged from the privations of war, and they greeted Dior's extravagance with undisguised relief while male politicians were busy denouncing it. Fashion magazines have had almost as much influence as the designers. Braving puritan mockery, they still set standards which millions of women eagerly accept. As Dorothy Parker said in 1915, when she was working for American *Vogue*: "We couldn't have bought a Paris handkerchief, but that didn't deter us from enlightening Mrs Vanderbilt on the fashion she was to follow." Later, she could have phrased it a little differently: ". . . as to the fashion she *should* follow."

Modern art was important as well. Whether praised, misunderstood or simply ridiculed, it influenced everybody's attitude. In 1913, an American critic denounced Van Gogh's paintings as rubbish. By 1935, 26,000 visitors had flocked to the Museum of Modern Art to see an exhibition of his work.

Throughout the period which is surveyed here, Paris indisputably led the way in all things elegant. Foreign buyers purchased both outfits and photographs, and these were afterwards copied everywhere. In the early days women, amongst them the very wealthy, simply set their maids or local seamstresses to work making versions of Paris models, often using fabrics which had been bought in Paris. This was true even of underwear. For this kind of work a dressmaker was paid about three shillings a day – about the cost of four yards of inexpensive silk. Yet a wealthy woman could easily spend, even at these rates, 100,000 francs a year on her clothes, and would perhaps run up another 200,000 francs in debts if she were really extravagant. In 1911, a visiting dress might cost between 800 and 1000 gold francs. A *déshabillé* would cost roughly the same, unless it came from a well-known fashion house, when it might cost up to 3000 francs. Fashionable hats could be found for 200 francs, but if they were adorned with bird-of-paradise plumes then the price could rise to 1500 francs.

Haute couture set standards which those with smaller incomes found it impossible to keep up. However, a few aids to economy were available. In more modest households, paper patterns were already in use at the turn of the century.

Where fashion information was concerned, there was for a long time conflict about the way in which it should be conveyed. A fashion journalist once told me that "women want dreams" – it was her reason for preferring to show idealised fashion plates rather than real clothes on real people. We must remember that, until quite recently, this dream element was indeed important. Millions of women were seduced by the glamour of Hollywood film-stars, and strove to look like them. Others, fewer perhaps and more sophisticated, submitted docilely to the dictatorship of the couturiers. Yet in some part of their minds all these women were aware that the enterprise was hopeless – their own physical imperfections, and their financial limitations too, would prevent them from achieving a true simulacrum of what they admired and tried to copy. Slavish imitation of glamorous and unattainable exemplars is now a thing of the past, and the designers' collective dictatorship is over, though their ideas are still a useful inspiration.

Fashion has become so diffuse that it serves the individual taste rather than trying to rigidly impose itself. Women are more sensible – or less desperate. Who would nowadays hop on a bike wearing uncomfortable wooden cups in order to try and make her bosom look more opulent? Who, on the contrary, would use flatteners, as they did in the twenties? The body is now allowed to express itself naturally. Yet one must not exaggerate. There were always those who were interested in regarding fashion with a steady eye, and who wanted to see it as it was. The Seebergers were the most indefatigable of these unbiased observers. The records they compiled are unlike any others, because they show exactly what fashion looked like, and how it was worn by those who claimed the leadership. What they bring us is no fairytale.

The Seebergers

The three brothers Seeberger – Jules, born in 1872; Louis, born two years later; and Henri, born in 1876 – had hardly completed their studies when their father died. The three boys had to earn a living and they chose to train as artists. As they were talented and hard-working, they received medals, prizes and grants and immediately found employment. Henri established his own studio in 1900. Jules was so fascinated by photography that he decided to turn professional and, with his brothers' help, photographed a series on various districts of Paris. The pictures were exhibited and made an impression. The three brothers all became photographers. In 1909, the magazine *La Mode Pratique* commissioned regular fashion contributions from them. Other magazines followed suit, among them *Les Modes*, *Le Jardin des Modes*, *L'Album du Figaro*, *Femina*, *L'Art et la Mode*, *Vogue*, and *Harper's Bazaar*. Jules retired in 1926 because of ill-health and his brothers stopped working in 1939. Of the three brothers, only Louis had married. His two sons, Jean and Albert, had started working with their father and uncle in 1927 and 1930 respectively. They took over the family business in 1939. During the war, they worked under great stress – they stopped attending the elegant gatherings and concentrated on outdoor and studio fashion photography with professional models. Some of the family silverware was bartered for essential laboratory ingredients. Jean and Albert Seeberger have now retired, retaining numerous fond memories of their working years and of the models they liked best: Fabienne, Bettina, Anne Campion, Sophie and Simone.

1909

Perfect Summer elegance – straw hat with
bird of paradise, lace, parasol and silk flowers.

The rules of society were as rigid as the structure of a woman's dress, created primarily by an 'S'-shaped, laced and boned corset, thought of as a health corset. An American painter, Charles Dana Gibson, immortalized the ideal beauty of this era as the 'Gibson girl': uplifted prominent bosom, tight and sinuous waist, and an equally prominent bottom. Her hair was piled up and padded with 'rats'. Gibson's chief model was his own wife, who had two equally attractive sisters. One of them later became Lady Astor.

In 1907, Lucile, an audacious *femme du monde* turned couturière, well known for her sophisticated gowns of soft materials, had designed a huge hat worn by Lily Elsie in *The Merry Widow* – and two years later it was still very much in fashion.

Actresses often modelled couturiers' clothes for magazines as well as wearing them on stage, thus acting as trend-setters. Maxine Elliott, star of the American and London theatres, would spend up to $1000 on one dress. The fashion houses had until recently shown their outfits to clients on dummies but, after Worth had started presenting his clothes on live models (who wore tight black garments underneath), Lucile went one step further and introduced fashion *défilés*, giving each item a name.

The wardrobe of a lady included a vast number of dresses and coats, as she was expected to change about five times a day and could not be seen wearing the same clothes too often. There were morning outfits, those for shopping, for visiting in the afternoon, for various outdoor social gatherings, and for evening receptions. A fashionable woman would have up to eight furs and a whole range of accessories, including a number of fans – a must for theatre and receptions – and summer parasols.

Looking after this wardrobe, even the priceless jewellery, was her maid's

responsibility – a girl earning less than £30 a year. There was no shortage of domestic help: easily a dozen servants would be employed in the service of a family of five or six. In country houses, where the summer season was very lively, there could be thirty, plus some gardeners, to look after the family and their guests. Marriage was the only way out of service for a working girl, unless she could sew well, as opportunities of earning an honest living were scarce.

Entertaining was considered a basic way of life and was run on a virtually industrial scale. The Duchesse de Gramont is said to have entertained some 90,000 guests in her lifetime! Fashion was largely addressed to the mature woman. Among the best houses in Paris were Worth (an Englishman), Callot Sœurs, Madame Paquin, Lucile and Doucet. Fortuny, a Spaniard settled in Venice, was renowned for his finely pleated

tea-gowns inspired by Greek tunics. Tailored suits were a British speciality, with Redfern and Creed – established in Paris since 1850 – the favourites. Burberry made mainly outfits for sports like golf or motoring.

The use of the motorcar was gradually spreading: Ford had just launched his model T. The automobile was still considered a hazardous means of travelling, though not as dangerous as the fragile plane that wafted Blériot over the Channel. Few people saw a future for this eccentric new machine. As an industry, however, fashion was still in its infancy. Worth had started to sell some models to manufacturers and big stores, but mainly in the USA. There, Macy's had been open since 1858 and Neimann Marcus (owned by Herbert Neimann and his sister and brother-in-law Marcus) had been founded in 1907. However, elegant Americans still preferred to go to Paris for their clothes. *Vogue*,

already seventeen years old, kept its readers well informed about all social events, laid down the golden rules of good manners, and discussed the latest Paris fashions.

The most talented, daring and original couturier in Paris was Poiret, who had, since his début in 1904, launched a fierce campaign against the corset, and introduced the brassière. Of course, corsets were still being worn, but Poiret wanted the body to be free and look natural. This was a revolutionary idea. Poiret was always closely associated with avant-garde artists from whom he commissioned fabric patterns. The Fauves exhibition of 1905 was in step with his own taste for bright colours. Although often simple in cut, his dresses were enriched with oriental, exotic and Cubist patterns which gave them an exuberant look. When in 1909 Diaghilev brought to Paris his Ballets Russes, he caused an artistic and cultural tremor that

matched Poiret's aspirations, although he was jealous of the Russian impresario's success. Diaghilev gathered to him the most brilliant dancers, painters and musicians ever to work under one patron since the time of the Sun King, Louis XIV. Thanks to his alliance with the most advanced artistic circles, Poiret's influence was considerable and he never lacked publicity. Yet, he also met resistance from many wealthy and mature women – 'mature', in those days, meant from thirty onwards. Such women found it psychologically

and even physically impossible to part from their crippling corsets. Both minds and bodies were too accustomed to its constraint. Then, too, Monsieur Poiret's *laissez aller* had an air of lasciviousness hardly compatible with the strict, even harsh, conventions of their class. They still preferred the intricate embroideries, cobweb laces and frills they were used to, with a high neckline for day wear and a plunging *décolleté* revealing bare shoulders for the evening.

It is curious that, even as they protested against Poiret's innovations,

Sigmund Freud was lecturing in the USA and Mahler was completing his 9th symphony. For once, the intellectual and artistic ferment was alien to its contemporary surroundings. Between the world of experiment and that of convention, Poiret was one of the few to try to build a bridge.

1910

Not, we may assume, a French client.
She seems to lack elegance and chic.

A tailored suit aspiring to be a dress.
Unconventional for the time.

Typical salon, *where the mannequins had to present outfits at any time the clients arrived.*

Mais oui! *Straight from Feydeau. Boa, organdie, feathers, embroidery. She looks shy and naughty.*

The British were mourning Edward VII and welcoming their new king, the unexciting but deeply respectable George V. King Edward's reign had lasted only nine years, after a lifetime in his mother's shadow. Among other things, Victoria had not approved of Edward's taste for pretty women, music halls and gay company. Unable to resist the temptation of worldly pleasures he was not permitted to indulge at home, Edward used to cross the Channel to Paris, leaving behind his charming wife Alexandra – one of the truly elegant women of Victorian England. His incognito visits enhanced the reputation of Paris as the capital of all things sinful, elegant and exciting. The city was then at the height of the legendary Belle Epoque – those words evoke images of a scintillating, frivolous and easy-going life. Yet, many Parisians lived very differently. Leisure was obviously the privilege of the rich, although respectable families kept strictly within the rules of moral and social behaviour. These allowed

for a lot of gossiping, but not much fun. Sex was taboo, divorce a disgrace and the sight of an ankle very titillating. What gave flexibility to the situation was the existence of a double standard of morality. Women were goddesses and also playthings. Husbands approved of boring respectability if they were married to it, but it was approval without enthusiasm.

The fashionable man's true companion was the courtesan, scornfully nicknamed *cocotte*. Capricious, elegant, often beautiful, sometimes witty, such women gave light-hearted informal parties (to which respectable women were not invited) and made a living from adroitly managed love affairs. They were geishas rather than prostitutes and their favours cost both time and money. Some of the most famous – Emilienne d'Alençon, Cléo de Mérode and La Belle Otéro, all fierce rivals – could boast of keeping kings begging at their doors and of ruining many fortunes. They spent

lavishly on clothes or at the gambling-tables. Theatres, music halls, the races, casinos, fashionable cafés, and restaurants like Maxim's, were their domain, their field of battle. All the scandals concerning them were savagely reported by the satirical press. If the Belle Epoque was only truly enjoyed by a few, at least the echoes of it entertained the rest.

In 1910, the season was set alight by Diaghilev's two new ballets. *The Firebird*, the work of a young Russian composer of twenty-eight, Igor Stravinsky, with Fokine and Karsavina in the leading parts, was received with wild enthusiasm. Debussy rushed backstage to kiss the composer of such an unusual and talented score. *Sheherazade* followed, with a score by Rimsky-Korsakov, and with Ida Rubinstein as a divinely exotic harem creature and the great Nijinsky, of whom it was said that the ease displayed by this turbulent genius made him more aerial than mortal.

1911

An upper-class couple. He looks so
Edwardian that he could even be British.

Little by little Poiret's ideas were gaining ground. The elegant adopted his soft, long mantles and the apparent simplicity of his dresses. He achieved this look by first draping the fabric on the model to see how it fell most naturally. Most fashion houses had by now adopted tight bustles, high waistlines and supple, narrower skirts, rejecting bulky petticoats and 'Merry Widow' hats as too voluminous for the new silhouette. Short sleeves became usual but were complemented by gloves that hid the elbow.

Under Poiret's patronage, Raoul Dufy, until then a poor and unnoticed painter, became a successful fabric designer. He later observed that women who would not buy his paintings willingly wore his equally daring and colourful dress materials. Women began to tire, as Poiret said, of looking like decorated bundles and a few of them adopted overnight the boyish, flat-chested shape *Punch* was making fun of in 1911 in a cartoon captioned 'The Sex Question'. Changes, from now on, were to take place at an accelerated pace. Poiret, still innovating, created his own perfume and toured the European capitals with his models to present his creations and lecture on fashion.

In Paris, Cubism was already in progress. Juan Gris, Braque and Picasso were hard at work; Matisse, too, though his style was very different. Italy and Russia were at grips with Futurism. Vienna now had more to offer than Strauss's waltzes: Klimt's paintings, the music of Richard Strauss and Gustav Mahler. Both the *Rosenkavalier* and the *Song of the Earth* were written in 1911. Mahler, still only recognized by a few, died in the same year. In Munich, Franz Marc and Kandinsky founded the *Blaue Reiter*.

Parisians rushed to see Diaghilev's new ballet *Petrushka*, with music by Stravinsky and décor by Benois, which reflected their new enthusiasm for

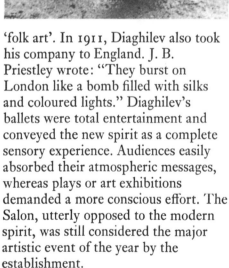

'folk art'. In 1911, Diaghilev also took his company to England. J. B. Priestley wrote: "They burst on London like a bomb filled with silks and coloured lights." Diaghilev's ballets were total entertainment and conveyed the new spirit as a complete sensory experience. Audiences easily absorbed their atmospheric messages, whereas plays or art exhibitions demanded a more conscious effort. The Salon, utterly opposed to the modern spirit, was still considered the major artistic event of the year by the establishment.

Fashion magazines like *Les Modes*, aiming at a conservative readership, tried to ignore the presence of Poiret and certainly made no reference to the new movements in art. Their illustrations were still very *art nouveau*, all in curves.

In the USA, where fortunes were more recent, society was less rigid and stratified than it was in Europe. New trends spread fast. The latest one was salon dancing. *Thés dansants* proliferated rapidly under the influence of a good-looking and energetic couple, Irene and Vernon Castle. The triumph of the foxtrot is an early example of innovation travelling from west to east: the Castles' European tour was a success that set the fashionable foxtrotting in no time.

Everywhere, the younger generation was showing an impatience for fun, novelty and speed that bicycling and hunt balls no longer fulfilled. Girls were not yet demanding freedom, but a certain hunger for sexual equality was in the air. Showing one's ankle had by now ceased to be indecent. Smart seaside resorts like Deauville were frequented. European titles were marrying American money, and high society was becoming less exclusive, with a greater emphasis on wealth than on birth. American girls were influential in creating a craze for sport. The British were also enthusiastic about outdoor activities, although, to the well-brought-up French girl, a walk or a game of croquet seemed strenuous enough.

1912

Hobble skirt, short-sleeved belted tunic –
and disapproving onlookers.

A bit of an Amazon and a little
eccentric: the hair style and the large
pendant are unusual.

China was undergoing its first political
change of the century in rejecting the
Manchurian imperial rule and
replacing it with a republic under Sun
Yat-sen, but Europe was not yet
alarmed by the ominous signs of
things to come.
The season started disastrously when,
on 15th April, news came of the loss of
the *Titanic*. She was on her maiden
voyage en route to New York and
among the passengers were many
international socialites eager to
experience the latest in modern
technology and luxury. Over 1500
passengers perished.
In America, industry was booming.
Grand Central Station was opened to
transport the whole of America to
New York. The United States was the
land of plenty, but sophisticated
Americans continued to spend their
money abroad. Lady Astor, an
American married to a man of
American origin, completely
identified herself with the English
upper classes.
Cinema had now entered the lives of
the masses. Silent films attracted five
million spectators a day. The French
inventors, the brothers Lumière, had
not foreseen the importance cinema
was rapidly going to gain. It was a
young art still waiting for its
masterpieces, but it was already
obvious that its impact on daily living,
and therefore on fashion, was going to
be considerable. Designers were
making more and more use of
modernist ideas. Duchamp
exhibited his *Nude Descending a
Staircase*, Brancusi sculpted his very
stylised pieces and Schönberg
produced *Pierrot Lunaire*.
In Paris, Lucien Vogel published the
first issue of *La Gazette du Bon Ton*,
a magazine attuned to the new trends.
In the choice of every detail, its small
format, its typeface, the quality and
tone of the paper and mainly the
youthful talent of the artists and the
subtlety of the hand-coloured plates,

Mole coat. She has the best money can buy and the assurance to go with it.

Beads and lace. The décolleté is covered up to the neck. The dress is asymmetric but not at all avant-garde.

Deauville early summer. The décolleté is covered by a bib of tulle fastened at the back of the neck.

each copy of the *Gazette* is a delight. It was created for the refined, elegant and modern young woman. There were no photographs, but much use was made of good illustrators, many first employed by Poiret for his catalogues. They included Barbier, Lepape, Marty, Martin, Iribe and Erté. Fashion and art have seldom been so intimately and successfully linked. The *Gazette* devoted itself to fashion and topics of essentially social and feminine interest, inevitably including texts on the Ballets Russes. Vogel was later to publish other fashion magazines, among them *Jardin des Modes. La Gazette* was bought by

Vogue in 1925 and thereafter disappeared.

A new fashion house was opened by Madeleine Vionnet. She had a good professional background, having worked for Doucet and Callot. The sensation of the season was again provided by Diaghilev's Ballets Russes performing *L'Après-Midi d'un Faune*, with music by Debussy, sets and costumes by Bakst, and choreography by Nijinsky, who also interpreted the central part. It caused a public outcry. An indignant *Figaro* wrote: "We have seen an indecent faun, expressing through vile gestures an erotic and heavily impure

bestiality." The sculptor Rodin replied in protest that harmony in this ballet was complete and reminiscent of the beauty of a Greek masterpiece. Nevertheless, a public apology was demanded from Diaghilev. Society did not mind the incursion of a decoratively sensual orientalism but was not quite ready to accept the display of anything so overtly and forthrightly sexual. The boudoir was acceptable, the faun was not.
The other creation of the season was *Daphnis and Chloe*, one of Ravel's masterpieces.

Finely pleated skirt with effect of braces and embroidered sailor collar. A young-looking summery outfit.

The French say 'too beautiful to be honest'. Indeed, the skirt is very near the body.

1913

*These three girls are models. They generally came
from modest families and had good moral references.*

This is quite daring – a mock evening suit. However, the supple drapes of the skirt give it a soft look.

Chrysanthemums in the brocade and in the bouquet, an obi-like belt and kimono sleeves: the influence of Japan.

The absence of make-up is obvious. Soft wool, big buttons everywhere. Hems, stitches and creases were often apparent.

Hobble skirts were now on their way out. Very narrow at the ankles, they had taken one graceful step farther the already straight lines of Poiret's skirts. They were also his idea, of course, as, for the time being, the other fashion houses were now following his lead. Hobble skirts were impractical, of course, as they restricted movement, but fashion was seldom concerned with the practical. With the decline of the cumbersome flared skirts – which had concealed pockets – handbags, purses, satchels and reticules became basic accessories. Clasps were of tortoiseshell or metal; pouches were of various types of silk fabric or of soft skins adorned with embroidery, beading or fringe trimming; the handle was often just a

length of silk cord. In winter, one could wear a muff with an inside pocket. Wealthy women did not need to carry much. They had charge accounts in shops, or their maids would pay the bills as they did not, in general, shop alone. They did not carry make-up either; this was still unacceptable and was considered the mark of easy virtue. Ladies did not use public transport, but were chauffeur-driven or occasionally they took a cab. (The Duc d'Harcourt had once ventured to try the new Paris *métro* but took a liveried footman who opened the carriage doors for him.) Hats, now much smaller, could not accommodate piled-up hair. Hair now framed the face in soft waves and was tied low on the neck in a bun, thus

producing a gentle effect which suited the supple drapes of the skirts. Permanent waving, invented in the USA, was still a painful and imperfect process and hair was seldom dyed. As they had taken to Irene Castle's foxtrotting, some women – mostly members of a small *coterie* – also took to her bobbed hair – quite a revolution, considering it had not been worn short since the eighteenth century. To the politically active, a rare species in France but vociferous in England, such details of appearance were irrelevant. The suffragette movement was growing increasingly militant under the leadership of Mrs Pankhurst, a woman of good social background who for ten years now had been fighting for the improvement of

women's rights. She had recently been imprisoned for inciting people to place explosives outside Lloyd George's house. She had resorted to violent action in order to shake up the indifference of a society based on male domination and female submissiveness. In a world of class segregation – wealth and power being synonymous – the working classes did not have many opportunities, except through strikes, of improving their lot – and working women least of all. One of the very few women's strikes, but a massive one, had been organised in the USA by girls in the needle trade whose working conditions in sweat shops were intolerable.

As women and fashion were on the path of rapid evolution, Proust, a recluse in his Parisian flat, was absorbed in writing *A la Recherche du Temps Perdu*, his literary monument to a way of life on the verge of disappearance. D. H. Lawrence's *Sons and Lovers* struck a more modern note, while Thomas Mann's *Death in Venice* and Alain Fournier's *Le Grand Meaulnes* expressed a sensitive romanticism.

Parisian society, as expected, rushed to see the première of Diaghilev's latest production, *The Rite of Spring*. So did most musicians in Paris, to whom Stravinsky's music was of tremendous interest. This time, though, both score

and choreography proved too advanced for most of the audience. Whether it was the pagan ritual in its audacious choreography or the strange and forceful sounds of the music that most shocked the public is still a matter for debate. Whatever the cause, the evening turned into a riot. Composers such as Ravel and Debussy knew they had witnessed an important musical event. For many others, including Saint-Saëns, who left before the end, the performance had been a scandal . . . one was better off watching Feuillade's *Fantômas*, showing at the cinema in five gripping episodes!

Diamanté shoe buckles, taffeta skirt in rows of petals. It is spring and life is gay.

This looks very complicated and must require a maid to help the assemblage.

During the first half of the year, a succession of alarming reports filled the newspapers day after day. Talk of war swept Europe. The European political situation had become increasingly disturbed by the military ambitions of the Great Powers. This was the case with the Russian anarchists and communists, who had to work in secret within Russia or live in exile. Lenin had left Russia in 1907 and was now busying himself all over Europe, organising Marxist militants. Industrial life, and conscription into standing armies, led workers everywhere to a political awareness not previously experienced among the peasants. The press had a monopoly as the channel of communication, but the intricacies of domestic politics – let alone the subtleties of foreign affairs – were little understood.

In New York, the first issue of *Harper's Bazaar* presented *Vogue* with a serious challenge. It appealed to a similar readership but this was large enough to secure a future for both magazines. *Vogue* had the advantage of being well known already for its high standards and the talent of its contributors. It was employing artists like Lepape (whose covers have in recent years successfully been reissued as posters). It had close connections with the rich élite of New York and the East Coast cities. True, there was wealth to be found around San Francisco, but *Vogue* did not consider the West Coast worthy of much attention. Determined to remain select, it mentioned only a few of the East Coast establishments selling the models it illustrated.

Not far from Los Angeles, in Hollywood, the cinema studios were expanding. Production was not yet perfected, and was not sufficiently powerful to impose its own restrictions upon the imaginative. Chaplin embarked on the first of a series of films featuring the clumsy, cunning, sentimental, perverse, ingenious,

pathetic little man trotting along in baggy trousers and bowler hat, swinging his cane as he walked – a figure which Chaplin's genius would make immortal.

In Western Europe, social life pursued its even courses, despite the threat of war and the rumblings of revolution. Hats lost their brims and became simple toques graced by a dash of tall feathers. Waists were nearly back in their rightful place.

Chanel, a relative newcomer, had recently opened premises in Deauville.

She was not entirely unknown, as she was already reasonably successful as a *modiste*. In fashion, she leaned towards the use of jerseys and simple clothes influenced by sportswear.

Then, on the 28th of June, the archduke Ferdinand of Austria and his wife were assassinated in the remote town of Sarajevo. Newspapers breathlessly reported a series of failed international meetings, ultimatums, mobilisations and finally declarations of war: the Austro-Hungarian empire went to war with Serbia, Germany

Beautifully cut tailored suit. The whole looks neat and witty.

Their name is Anglo-Saxon and they could be American, elegant and relaxed.

with Russia. On the 3rd of August, Germany declared war on France; Great Britain on Germany; Austria on Russia; France and Great Britain on Austria. It seemed like a chess-game gone mad.

Canadian contingents arrived in England. British troops soon landed in France and, before the end of August, the Germans had invaded the north of France after sweeping through Belgium. Men departed in their thousands, leaving behind work that still had to be done. Ammunition factories needed many hands. Women were left to fend for themselves. Apart from working in factories, there was not a great deal civilians could do – and the upper classes were not expected to take on the dirty jobs. Willing ladies set up charity balls or parties and held knitting sessions in the afternoon. Of course, fashion was affected by the cataclysm. A smart woman would wear 'horizon blue' similar to that of the French troopers' uniforms and opt for a sober look. She might correspond with a lonely officer (simple soldiers would not do). Everyone felt intensely patriotic.

Madeleine Vionnet decided to close her fashion house for the time being, but the American buyers remained constant even as the German advance was threatening Paris itself.

25

1915~18

*The looks are serious, hems are going up
and the dress is made of soft wool.*

*Simple elegance, discretion and
refinement. It works so much better than
a surplus of ornaments.*

*A lucky one who is not in mourning.
Black would have been compulsory and
clothes were dyed in a day.*

As 1915 drew to a close, hopes of ending the war in a matter of months had vanished. War casualties, already heavy, did not spare the civilians. There were Zeppelin raids over London and Paris. Nearly 1200 passengers were missing after the Germans had sunk the *Lusitania*. Shelling had destroyed large areas of Belgium and the north and east of France. War propaganda raged on all sides. The German engineer, Junker, built the first all-metal plane, faster and tougher than its wood-and-fabric opponents. A large part of Europe, stretching as far as Turkey, had been turned into a battlefield. Tanks made their first appearance. Political unrest increased sharply, with riots in Moscow and the Easter rebellion in Ireland. Rasputin, said to be the true ruler of Russia through the malevolent and magnetic influence he exercised over the Czar's family, was murdered by a group of young aristocrats. In 1916, the German troops launched their first assault on Verdun. Its name was to become the symbol of four years of pitiless and massive slaughter. The USA, not yet involved, were strongly sustaining the Allies' military effort.

Links between New York, London and Paris were strong. Charity shows were held in New York for the benefit of the French fashion industry. American life was maintaining its pace. Two major films were released: *Birth of a Nation* by Griffiths and *The Tramp* by Chaplin. Mary Pickford emerged as the ideal heroine of the silent movies – an embodiment of purity and innocence. The jazz craze was taking all the night-clubs by storm.

What was left of Parisian society? Some of its members retreated to their country residences. Others turned theirs into hospitals or convalescent homes for soldiers, if they had not already been requisitioned. Most families had relatives at the front, many were already mourning them. Daughters and sisters took up social work or nursing. Social classes were for a time united by sorrow.

The aged Monet was painting his Water Lilies in isolation and near blindness. Feuillade went on filming *Judex*, in twelve episodes.

Dresses were shorter – well above the ankles. Women wore soft wool in the morning, velvet in the afternoon; satins, tulles and muslin were for evening dresses, all in harmonies of pale colours. Coats were made of thick fabric and fur trimmings were added everywhere. The mood was not frivolous.

1919

*Gaiety breaks out again. The dress is probably
silk jersey but it could by now be rayon.*

*Light drapes of printed chiffon. The hem
has dropped and gloves are no longer
compulsory in summer.*

Throughout 1917 and 1918, the
Seeberger brothers served in the army
so there is a gap in our documentation.
But these two terrible years cannot be
omitted.

1917 was the most murderous of the
war. The stress and appalling
conditions in the trenches led to
mutinies. Between their intervention in
late June 1917 and the armistice of
November 1918, the Americans lost
81,000 men. The British royal family,
who had close European links,
renounced its German name and
titles. There were mutinies of a more
directly political character in the
German and Russian fleets. At length,
full-scale revolution erupted in Russia
It caused great emotion throughout
Europe, where people recalled the
French Revolution of 1789.

In Paris, society life was still very
lively, so much so that the government
banned jewels and evening dresses at
the opera and appealed to the public
not to buy new dresses.

Women had adopted barrel shirts.
Bobbed hair, cut short, was now worn
in factories because it was safer. It also
suited the American way of life,
although Theda Bara, coined as the
first vamp, made it look far from
sporty.

Diaghilev presented a Cubist ballet,
Parade, with sets and costumes by
Picasso. For these the poet Apollinaire
invented the term 'Surrealist', later to
be used in a rather different sense.

Dixieland, by 1918, had travelled to
Europe with the black American
soldiers. Chic Parisians took to the
new music.

Russia had been knocked out of the
conflict and there was now a bitter
civil war between 'Reds' and 'Whites'.
The Allies, not disposed in 1919 to
tolerate the new Bolshevik régime, sent
troops to Russia in aid of the Czar and
his 'white' supporters. His assassination
and that of his family was felt by
many to be even more shocking than
the number of soldiers killed every day.

Famine and typhus claimed millions of Russians.

For Germany, November 1918 was the end. Revolution, led by the Communist group Spartacus, had broken out in Berlin. Kaiser Wilhelm II had abdicated and a humiliating armistice had been signed with the Allied forces. At last the war was over.

Millions of people, overwhelmed with joy and relief, poured into the streets to give the returning troops a delirious welcome. Yet, the trauma had been such that many of the survivors were left with haunting nightmares for the rest of their lives. Fatal casualties amounted to nearly one and a half million Frenchmen and well over that figure for Germany and Russia. Britain mourned 800,000 dead from the British Empire.

Britain was also suffering from a lethal epidemic of influenza, the 'Spanish flu'. Similarly drastic outbreaks of the disease took place on the Continent. But by 1919, Paris had regained its lead in all arts but the cinema. As a member of *Tout Paris* said: "Art cannot flourish without a wealthy and leisured class to savour it." He believed the pleasures of art should remain in the hands of a happy few. Democratisation of the arts was still a long way off, and it was the wealthy who had the money and leisure to enjoy sport, which was now more fashionable than ever, especially golf, riding and tennis. Suzanne Lenglen's name appeared on every front page as the first French woman to win the Wimbledon lawn tennis championship. Sportswomen were concerned with the practicality of their clothes. Suzanne Lenglen's headband became famous.

Fashion in general was simple. Vionnet had reopened the previous year. Poiret, prosperous, launched his night-club 'l'Oasis', though he banned jazz from it. The dimly lit, refined oriental atmosphere proved so attractive that people flocked there on Friday nights – even in summer when no one would normally dream of spending the weekend in town.

With society life booming again, three new couturiers emerged: Molyneux, an Englishman who had worked with Lucile, Jean Patou and Lucien Lelong. Jeanne Lanvin, known for years as the best designer for young girls' clothes, had established herself during the war with a style popular among younger women for its romantic freshness.

Feathers had become less abundant. Ostrich, though, was much used on evening hats, glycerined so as to give the plumes the weight necessary for a droopy look. Diamonds could also be set in the rib of the feather. Paris was so much the centre of fashion that, as incredible as it may sound now, the time lag between Paris and educated England was about twelve years. Upper-class women like Lady Astor, who had become the first female Member of Parliament in London, dressed in Paris or had their maid copy Paris models, using French fabrics. Only Lady Astor's tailored suits were made in London.

The war had caused an economic crisis. The working class, aware of the importance of their contribution, longed for improvements. Welcomed home as heroes, many soldiers found they could not find employment. Their frustration and bitterness found two channels: communism and fascism.

1920

After Carmen, here is Don José. A lot of Chantilly lace, a top of printed panné velvet with a touch of monkey trimming. It might not be as chic as it is memorable. Signed Charlotte and Germaine.

In this year, fashion seemed to have entered a period of confusion. Hats were fan-like, *bretons*, or boat-shaped, turbans, cloches. There was the same variety in shoes – laces and ribbons, buckles and straps, although the latter dominated. Among the outfits illustrated here are a coat and a poncho dress which would not have been out of place in a fifties collection. But a clear tendency does emerge from the study of the leading couturiers' work, although they were trying to evolve in different directions. One must keep in mind that they were presenting up to 400 outfits in a single collection. The waist was now in place, but a little loose. There were some indications of a lower line, mostly on evening dresses, but it was not yet on the hip or vanished altogether. Evening dresses began to have bare backs and shoulder-straps. As for dresses worn on particularly elegant afternoon occasions, these could drop to the feet, but the usual length remained at half-calf level. Worth designed an evening dress of that length with a back panel forming the train.

Thanks to a more casual way of life, less ostentatious, informal two- or three-piece jersey outfits – Chanel's trademark – became the usual day wear, at first criticised for looking too poor. Most couturiers, in creating sober designs, were in danger of repeating themselves so they tried a number of variations. There were some hoop effects, obtained by gathering the fabric at the front or on the hips, from where it hung in waves of contrasting material. Skirts made to look like petals were one of Vionnet's successes. More was achieved in detail than in basic cut: fur trimmings – black monkey in particular – on summer dresses, embroidery on lapels and cuffs, fine lace over taffeta. Chanel is credited with introducing quilting, but Poiret may well have used it first on coats, if only for details. Designers made much use of printed fabrics of all kinds, and firms like Bianchini-Férier had a wide range as well as a good choice of woven patterns. They were using imaginative artists who could create anything from classic to floral and stylised to abstract. Jewellery had adopted a style appropriate to the simpler look: geometric shapes for the diamanté clips – essential to fasten a *décolleté* crossing over the bust or to hold the fold of a drape; simple linear brooches enriched by a large central pearl or precious stone; long strings of pearls or silken cords holding carved jade pendants.

The potential of a relatively new synthetic thread – rayon – was now being exploited. The Americans were manufacturing eight million pounds of it per year. Rayon was soft and shiny, quite strong and easily dyed, and it was much cheaper than silk but had a similar look. It was mainly used for jersey dresses and jumpers but it was starting to revolutionise the stocking industry. So far, elegant legs had worn

33

black or white silk and the others,
cotton. Most would soon be sporting
shades of beige.

The younger set enjoyed sports cars,
met at private parties or night-clubs,
went to the country at weekends, to
Deauville or Biarritz in summer and
also to the Riviera – hitherto a winter
resort. Girls were no longer
chaperoned. Anglo-Saxon influence
was noticeable on the Continent –
young people dropped the odd English
word, drank cocktails and thought jazz
was everything. They were fascinated
by the USA, where life had a much
faster rhythm: there were nearly nine
million cars there against hardly more
than half a million in France or
England. More and more exciting
things were coming from across the
Atlantic: films, new sounds and
dances. Paul Whiteman's jazz band
had toured Europe with enormous
success. Jazz had become the craze at
all social levels, in dance halls, on the
gramophone. It was going to spread
even more now that the first radio
stations had started broadcasting in the
USA and parts of Europe. The erotic
vitality of jazz corresponded perfectly
to the febrile thirst for mindless
oblivion. It was a normal post-war
reaction. But on a higher cultural level,
Anglo-Saxon influence was still
minimal, despite the nucleus of
brilliant personalities who had already
settled in Paris. Among them was
Gertrude Stein, portrayed by Picasso
as long ago as 1907.

In giving their women the right to
vote, the Americans were not pioneers:
the English (over thirty) and Germans
were a few years ahead of them and
the Norwegians, who had been able to
vote since 1907, had done even better.
Yet, French women would have to
wait another twenty-five years,
although they were popularly supposed
by foreigners to take many liberties –
at least in their private lives. This
assumption was not entirely true. What
they did possess was femininity,

Paniers do not work too well with a short skirt and kimono sleeves. By Doucet.

These two bizarre panels of rug separated by an inverted pleat make a summer dress.

Tailored suit by Creed, with one button only. The waistcoat lapel is worn over the jacket.

charm, a great deal of coquetry and the art of being courted. French women were not prettier than any others but could easily appear more attractive. It was part of their upbringing to take great care of their looks and be critical of themselves as well as of others. French *haute couture* would not have reached such high standards had it not had to please these difficult customers. The combination gave Paris its continuing influence over fashion, despite the adoption of trends from elsewhere. *Vogue* was putting a French edition on the market.

During the season, Diaghilev presented

Pulcinella, a ballet by Stravinsky who, this time, wrote a classically inspired score. Music-hall was flourishing and Maurice Chevalier, as the archetype of the hedonistic Parisian male, was a big success. Colette had long abandoned music-hall to pursue a literary career into which she carried both her talent and her ambiguous reputation. She had published *Chéri*, morally hardly more commendable than her previous books, too daring to be left in the hands of young persons.

If sexual liberty meant anything, it was limited to the very few who were able to place themselves above social rules.

As for the others, they did not know that they wanted it or knew they could not afford the stain of a bad reputation. Discreet affairs, however, could be pursued, provided one was married. The romanticism and indeed the sheer sentimentality of popular books and films did, however, indicate the presence of sexual fantasies needing an outlet. Women, in particular, were avid for sentiment. The war had drastically cut down the number of potential husbands and unless she had a comfortable dowry, a girl's chances were much reduced. The great romance of the year took

This coat could have been worn in the fifties. It is surprisingly modern and so is the turban hat.

Ensemble of soft textured wool trimmed with fox by Callot. The outline is outstanding.

place in Hollywood, when Mary Pickford married the dashing Douglas Fairbanks. This was film romance moving into real life. For the most part, real life was not what people expected from the movies: they knew these figures were remote from the ordinary world, but the public liked them because of their fantasy. Made-up vamps caught in the tangles of dramatic love affairs were rarely seen other than in luxurious dresses or

fancy costumes of theatrical inspiration. Gloria Swanson in this respect dominated the screen. She was the super vamp, the woman of fatal beauty and destiny. Another type of heroine was the poor little innocent girl. She was drawn, the victim of unscrupulous villains, into a repeated series of perilous adventures. She would be saved in the end by the chivalrous hero, love would triumph in a last embrace and the pair would

no doubt marry and live happily ever after. Another genre was the pseudo-historical, with Cleopatra as a favourite, as this allowed a lot of cardboard exoticism and masses of spectacular costumes. Needless to say, history was treated with the utmost freedom. On the whole, female roles were predominant except in the comic sketches. The major comic performers survive even when we see their work today. Chaplin had a rival in Buster

nationhood. Most of their compatriots were more parochial in their interests. To many, the really bad news was the newly imposed prohibition – a complete ban on alcohol. Not a drop of it was allowed in public or private premises. The dark age of prohibition had started, and it drove many citizens into illegal activities and allowed gangsterism to flourish into such a profitable industry that ruthless competition became inevitable. The speakeasy became an even more exciting place than the old-fashioned night-club.

Keaton, who established himself from the start as the man who never smiled. He used similar burlesque situations but had a more pessimistic approach. America needed both dreams and fun. One and a half million workers walked out in a succession of strikes – the manifestation of general economic unrest. The situation in Europe was even worse: France had a million and a half strikers and England two million. There is not much in common between the minority of those who could make pleasure their main pursuit and the majority to whom life was a constant struggle. Yet, popular imagery would have us believe that 1920 was a happy, fun-laden year. As far as America was concerned, the tone of the time was best reflected in the writing of men like O'Neill and Sinclair Lewis. They understood the stresses of the period, but balanced it with a new consciousness of

1921

This woman of great charm was one of Poiret's faithful clients. Here, a Spanish inspired outfit.

Silk dress by Chanel, although it looks very Vionnet.

38

Subtle match: discreet check for the floating panels, stripes for the jacket and plain skirt by Jenny.

Dior's 'A' line already? The horizontal stripes are bias ribbons.

1921 was not a very eventful year. Peace was back for good, there to be enjoyed. Only a handful of pessimists were worried that the conditions imposed on Germany were too harsh and could lead to yet another war, but war was something nobody wanted to talk about. Germany had been compelled to pay heavy war damages that would keep the country busy and tame for a long time. The United States, Great Britain, France and Italy had their own economic worries and when the German government proclaimed a state of emergency in the face of an economic crisis, this pleased the public rather than alarmed it: they felt the defeated Germans deserved the troubles they had brought on themselves. Europe increasingly turned to America for new entertainment. Jazz bands of black Americans were proliferating, as they were a must in fashionable night-clubs.

The glitter of Paris was attracting more and more Americans – artists, writers, or socialites fleeing the inconveniences of prohibition. Montparnasse on the south – or left bank – of the Seine was, like northern Montmartre, one of the areas of Paris in which painters and sculptors had chosen to live. It was also becoming the centre of the new American colony – people could live there cheaply and be within walking distance of the Seine and the rue de Fleurus where Gertrude Stein reigned over a circle of artists. A young American could always be sure of finding a familiar face in one of the cafés or night-clubs; acquaintances in wealthier circles would provide him with pleasant suppers and give him the chance of mingling with society. Invitations for weekends might follow. He might even be lucky enough to find a girl friend with her own sports car.

Parisian night life had become more adventurous. The growing fashion was to end the evening in parts of town where the sight of evening dress was somewhat unusual: to go to *les Halles* for a late supper, to drink onion soup among a crowd of blood-spattered meat porters or to make an expedition to one of the ill-famed dance-halls in slum areas where smart women would for a while swap their usual escorts for excitingly seedy but picturesque local characters whom they hoped were pimps or gangsters. Of course, such women would never dream of going anywhere near these areas in daylight. Excitement was all, exoticism was in. Hollywood launched Rudolf Valentino, whose handsome Latin looks turned him into the idol of millions of women. As The Sheik in the film of the same title or the tangoing hero of *The Four Horsemen of the Apocalypse*, his appeal was not so remote from that of the Parisian mobsters, who also treated women as women, not ladies. Films also reflected the appetite for

amusement and showed increasingly liberated behaviour as far as the female characters were concerned. Some Hollywood silents seem remarkably daring even today.

Fashion was gently evolving. In most cases, women seemed happy enough to leave their waist in place, but hems dropped slightly for elegant occasions, and shoes were mainly strapped. Lanvin launched the Aztec collection. Poiret, no longer the great sensation, still used beautifully rich fabrics, while Worth and Molyneux remained faithful to pure elegance.

One of the most interesting couturières was Vionnet, now imposing her sophisticated style. Her dresses were quite simple in appearance but very elaborate in cut. She was a master of cross-cutting and, instead of the usual straight hemline, preferred to let the points of fabric hang quite low. This effect of uninterrupted drape was

39

Dress by Poiret. The fabric could have been designed by Dufy and the long pendant is typical.

Buttonless ample cape-jacket trimmed with monkey by Drecoll.

unusual and was readily adopted by others. Vionnet was very sensitive about copying and had each of her creations photographed in front of a three-fold mirror. The model thus shown on every side would then be patented.

Artistic events were well reported in society magazines like *Vanity Fair*, *Harper's Bazaar* and *Vogue*. In New York, *Vogue*, conscious of the evolution in the arts and in photography, carried regular features by writers as distinguished as Virginia Woolf and Aldous Huxley. The photographs were frequently the work of the baron De Meyer or Steichen, men who were turning fashion photography into an art. Man Ray, just thirty, a friend of Duchamp and close to the Dada group, had arrived in Paris where he photographed Poiret's models, among others, while developing his own techniques of surrealist photography.

1922

The waist is much lower and Drecoll still favours monkey trimmings.

The romantic heroine of the early twenties, hidden by the large brim and a gracious cape.

1922 – and the low waistline typical of the twenties had been definitively adopted. It imposed a linear, supple and apparently simple look. Although there were no curves, and busts started to disappear, the look managed to appear feminine. With their short hair, shingled and now sometimes permed in soft waves, women looked younger – and they needed youth, since they now led strenuous lives, opening their own businesses, dancing, practising sports, travelling indefatigably and entertaining as much as society women did.

The discovery of Tutankhamen's tomb in Egypt – a major archaeological find – provided a brief pretext for dressing up in a pharaonic manner, complete with head-dress. Fashion houses were on the whole anxious to decorate so straight a line. Tunics or tabards were ideal – sleeveless, embroidered, worn over dresses of contrasting tones or, cross-cut, made to look like ponchos. Most garments had a horizontal, bare neckline. The hemline could not make up its mind whether to rise or fall. Enveloping capes were very becoming, wrapped around tubular dresses. They brought an elegant touch of soft mystery. Poiret, who had originated them as early as 1909, was happy with this fashion. The accent was on folklore, peasant embroidered patterns adapted to suits and dresses or batik printing on silk muslin.

Women wore cloche hats with casual short afternoon clothes and sportswear, or else romantic *capelines* low on the forehead with longer, more dressy outfits. This obliged them to raise their heads with a gracious swan-like movement of the neck. Parties were thriving, and now began late in the afternoon. The latest affairs and the newest titbits of gossip would be discussed over a variety of cocktails. Serious topics, such as unemployment and the first British hunger marches, or the Chinese civil war, were not considered to be very

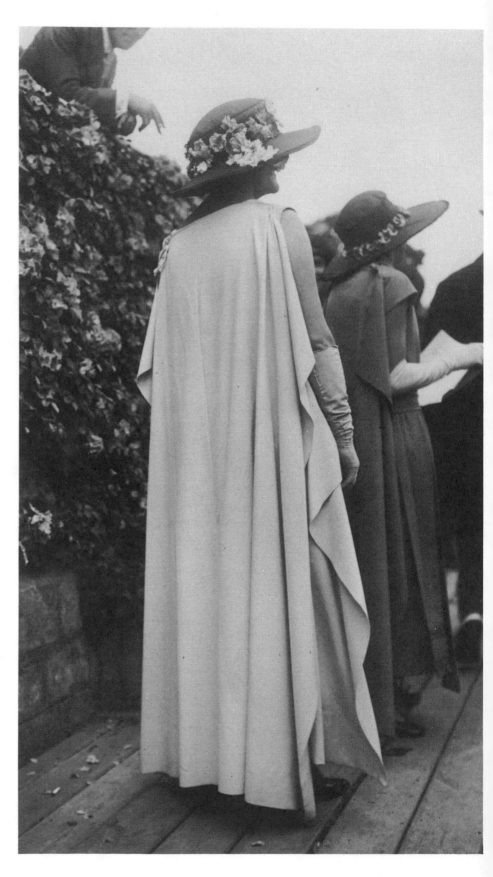

Elaborate silk dress: the asymmetrical panel cut across is sewn to the dress at the neck and shoulders.

Below left: Egypt revisited. Centre: velvet cut-across poncho, lined and trimmed with satin.

Right: an harlequinade that would have looked pretty in a drawing by Lepape.

interesting to the partygoers, but rumours of fights between socialists and fascists in Italy after Mussolini's seizure of power provided them with more excitement. The *Duce* could be seen gesticulating in newsreels at the cinema, but audiences soon forgot him, absorbed in the first scenes of *The Prisoner of Zenda*, starring Ramon Novarro, the latest of Hollywood Latin lovers.

Although he was no longer the revolutionary of his early years, Poiret had retained his popularity and kept his taste for byzantine luxury that suited his eccentric nature so well. The

attraction of the season was the spectacular Colonial Exhibition, set in a number of pavilions, each in the style of a different colony. Apart from Cambodia, Indo-China, Tahiti and the French islands of the West Indies, the French colonies were mainly located in Western and Northern African territories. For the first time, a large public was discovering the art of the primitive tribes which had, until then, been left to the attentions of the army and missionaries. It was a revelation and – for society at least, avid as it was for new sensations – the crude and grotesque, yet somehow magical and

sophisticated, ritual masks and wooden statues of the tribesmen came as a profound cultural shock. Negro art had already influenced Cubism. Now it was to have its effect on fashionable decorators and finally on the public at large. Society was catching up with the experiments made by contemporary artists. Furniture and interior design became more geometric, banning curves, and leaving bare large areas for space and light. The majority of the public still preferred flowers, stripes and gentle colours, but beige, off-white, brown and black pleased the fashionable.

Glass and chromed metal furniture were adopted by the most avant-garde people, those who also chose sculptures by Laurens or Brancusi, paintings signed Klee, Léger, Juan Gris, Kandinsky, Braque, Picasso and Delaunay. They read *Ulysses* by James Joyce, a difficult writer but a lord of language. Americans were talking about Dos Passos and Sinclair Lewis's *Babbitt*, while in England Stanley Spencer was emerging strongly from the new generation of painters, and D. H. Lawrence wrote *Women in Love* which for a while eclipsed the Bloomsbury group.

In Russia, the revolution had allowed a ferment of creativity to blossom, of which the West was not fully aware. Prokofiev had written his opera *The Loves of Three Oranges* the previous year, but he wrote it in the USA, where he had been living since 1918.

1923

Very embroidered, this dress by Amelina does not look heavy if worn, as here, by a tall handsome girl.

Full length for very elegant afternoons. Large hats, pearls by the yard. It is a fashion for slim women.

Typical Vionnet craftsmanship. The dress is in graduated tones. Diamanté pendant at the hip.

Jazz persisted, but a sinister note rumbled beneath the popular rhythms. The condition of Germany worsened. Unable to cope, Germany stopped making the enormous repayments imposed by the Allies at the end of the war – France and Belgium retaliated by occupying the Saar, seat of the steel industry. This aggravated the already ailing economy and brought further humiliation to the country. French economic boycott followed German passive resistance, making things worse. There were strikes, riots, martial law. A fantastic level of inflation had made the currency valueless: a single pound sterling would buy ten thousand marks. The communist uprising of the previous years had not reached the point of national revolution. Frustration and discontent led people to search for new hope and they started to rally in sympathy with the National Socialist party of Adolf Hitler, who attempted a *coup* in Munich and failed.

Meanwhile, similar movements were forming in other parts of Europe and all non-fascist parties had been banned in Italy.

However, a devastating earthquake in Japan did more to captivate public imagination than political tremors.

To some of the unfortunate Russians who had fled to Paris after the October revolution and who were now reduced to driving taxis, life offered a future of nostalgic yesterdays. In New York, prohibition was abandoned as totally unsuccessful and it was progressively ignored in many other states. It had brought more harm to the country than alcoholism ever would. Any determined drinker could always find a bottle. Smugglers, clandestine distillers, and the gangsters who controlled the black market and ran gambling houses and night-clubs at the same time, had all amassed fortunes. Prohibition had added a touch of excitement to night life, but brought corruption into the police force.

Quilted suit by Lanvin that looks simple but has refined stitch-work.

A Callot outfit at Deauville. The top could be worn today.

She looks more handsomely masculine than the man standing by. Note the large diamond bracelet and ankle chain.

The black Americans – marvellous players, singers and dancers – were enjoying an even greater vogue: no party was complete without them, either playing or demonstrating new dance steps. *Shuffle Along*, the first of several all-black shows, opened on Broadway, and Hollywood produced many films full of traditional black characters as seen by the whites. The best remembered is probably King Vidor's *Hallelujah*. Blacks were supreme entertainers, kings of rhythm and blues in a style inimitable by those who did not have African roots and that combination of sadness, faith and sarcastic humour that only generations of hopeless misery could engender. Behind the glitter lay the facts of segregation and the social deprivation. Would Bessie Smith have died after a car accident if the nearest hospital had not been for whites only?

Scott Fitzgerald, brilliant representative of his generation, had already written *Tales of the Jazz Age* and was living it out to the full with his pretty wife Zelda and many friends on both sides of the Atlantic. In Paris, the *Revue Nègre* had opened and everyone was rushing to see the star of the show, the beautiful Josephine Baker. She appeared with her long, harmonious, elastic body covered with wrist and ankle bracelets, wearing a loincloth and a belt of fake bananas, her shiny hair flattened with white of egg. Never had the *Folies Bergères* show had such splendid reviews. Josephine became overnight the most sought-after woman in town, the object both of admiration and of curiosity. Few blacks were then living in Europe and discrimination did not as yet exist against them. New York and Paris both had much to

offer, but the latter continued to be the centre of high fashion. In London, Norman Hartnell had opened his own house, but he had to wait several years – until, in fact, he presented his show in Paris – before he really established himself.

Now that waists had dropped, fashion paused for a while, making detailed improvements to the tubular look. Chanel had become a favourite, thanks to the practical simplicity of her casual clothes. Unlike her rivals, she had consistently opted for shorter skirts for all times of day, which made her outfits easy to spot, particularly in the evening.

Since the tubular dress looked best on slim women, the ever-present fight against weight began in earnest and spawned a specialised new industry, sometimes rather dubious in its practices. Gymnastics, physical jerks,

Lined hand printed asymmetrical tunic in one panel with matching scarf over a pleated dress by les Tissus d'Art.

massage, tablets and special diets – desperate women tried them all in succession.

The south of France, from the Italian border to Cannes, now attracted an increasing number of visitors and residents. The time to go was no longer the winter, but in full summer when the sun was at its hottest. Lovely villas overlooking the Mediterranean, often built in secluded spots among pine trees, eucalyptus and mimosa, had access to nearby beaches or picturesque little ports convenient for the mooring of visiting yachts. Driving from Cap Martin to Cannes was easy and one could stop on the way at Cap d'Antibes to lunch with friends. Monte Carlo was still the smartest and most famous casino in the world. There was a strong Anglo–Saxon settlement in the area, as Nice had for a long time been a favourite retreat for English people who could not readjust to the British climate after years of service in the tropics. Pretty Provençal villages, good food and excellent wines added to the attraction of the warm climate ideal for swimming and sun-bathing. Only older ladies (to whom a tanned complexion only signified years of outdoor menial work) objected to this new love of the sun and were still careful to protect themselves with large straw hats and parasols. The older generation also disapproved of the new revealing swimming costumes and the outrageous liberties taken by younger women.

Those who could afford golden memories turned these years into a legendary store of fun-loving and youthful summer days. The roaring twenties were sailing on full steam.

1924

*Important fur trimming for this coat by Paquin,
which is fastened low inside the lapel.*

The tempo was getting faster all the time. High society continued to play its part as the catalyst of artistic creativity. Ideas travelled rapidly from one party to another. Projects could be discussed during leisurely weekends in the country or in dimly lit night-clubs. The role of wealthy patrons was essential. They entertained in style and supported artists brought to their attention by clever go-betweens whose flair and *savoir faire* were not their only talents. Cocteau – artist, poet, writer and later film-maker – has left enough to be remembered by, but was probably even more important as a privileged messenger of the arts, a go-between *emeritus*, aesthete and dilettante whose sensitive antennae were as vital to the Parisian life of the time as the butterfly which pollinates the flowers. In 1924 he wrote the scenario of *Le Train Bleu*, produced by Diaghilev. This ballet, a danced operetta, showed the blend of talents that gave Paris such vitality: choreography – Nijinska; music – Darius Milhaud; curtain – Picasso; sets – the sculptor Henri Laurens – and costumes by Chanel.

After the show, *le Boeuf sur le Toit* was the place to spend the rest of the night, or perhaps *le Café de Paris*, near the Opéra. *Le Boeuf sur le Toit*, literally 'the Ox on the Roof', a surrealistic name already reminiscent of Chagall's flying goats, was conveniently situated just round the corner from the Théâtre des Champs-Elysées where all the Diaghilev and other avant-garde productions were presented. Another favoured meeting place was *la Closerie des Lilas*, considered the most pleasurable meeting ground in the Montparnasse area.

Skirts were going up and bosoms had vanished – over-endowed women were even flattening them. Chanel was making great use of long necklaces, and imposing costume jewellery on to

A pretty dress that seems cut out of a huge scarf.

Black and white sleeveless dress with pearl embroidery and matching appliqué for the muslin cape by Alice Herbin.

Suit by Jane with a very long jacket and hanging fur trimming

customers accustomed to wearing nothing but genuine stones. "It doesn't matter if they are real," she said, "as long as they look like junk."
Fur trimmings, never out of fashion, were much in evidence, particularly on coats, which were now buttonless and wrapped around the body as capes had been the previous year. But this made bags difficult to carry, so women took to flat wallets, which they slipped under the arm. Silk pyjamas marked a new trend. It was the first step towards wearing trousers, but were so far only intended as elegant *négligés*.
London was also very lively. Since they shared the same language, the British had closer links with America than the French. Bernard Shaw's

St. Joan was a great success; so was anything to do with Noël Coward. Coward and Cecil Beaton, who was establishing himself as one of the most talented photographers of his time, shared the role which in France belonged to Cocteau. Like Cocteau, Coward was adept at shocking people. Drugs, mostly opium or marijuana, were used by jazz musicians and also by a few curious people, eager to experiment with new sensations. *The Vortex* was the first play to show drug-taking. Though it was not necessarily illegal, there were public protests.
Broadway was ablaze with new shows. Gershwin's second important orchestral work, *Rhapsody in Blue*, was

well received. New York socialites, accustomed to clandestine expeditions since the prohibition era, now took to making incursions into all-black Harlem.
News came of the first talking films, a technical breakthrough that was to revolutionise cinema as an art and an industry. But not everyone who looked good on screen had a good voice. Some of the stars' vocal tests were disastrous. Many careers were threatened and panic spread among the Hollywood actors. What would happen to stars like the 'it' girl Clara Bow, who received 20,000 fan letters a week? Within a few years, there was an urgent need for proper scripts, elaborately written.

Shantung two-piece with very long chemise. Smocks at the shoulder and upholstered buttons.

Neat taffeta suit, propeller bow, ankle chain and fancy jewellery: this American has a very up-to-date elegance.

Lenin had died in Russia the year
before, leaving the country committed
to communism but in the hands of
disunited leaders. Russian cinema was
producing masterpieces of
revolutionary inspiration such as
Battleship Potemkin, based on the 1905
mutiny of the fleet at Odessa. The film
was acclaimed in Berlin the following
year.
Germany was still politically unstable
and deeply divided between
communism and emergent fascism.
Hitler, briefly gaoled as a

trouble-maker, wrote *Mein Kampf.*
But Germany had creative as well as
destructive forces. The Bauhaus,
founded by Gropius in 1919, was still
flourishing, Schönberg was teaching in
Berlin, and one of his best known
pupils, Alban Berg, had his own
Wozzek produced at the Berlin State
Opera, although, like Webern and
Kafka – who wrote *The Trial* that year
– he usually lived in Vienna.
London was reading *Mrs Dalloway,* a
remarkable novel by Virginia Woolf,
whose introspective talent expressed

itself in subtle impressionistic touches.
By now she was recognised as one of
the important writers of her time. The
group to which she belonged was
called 'Bloomsbury', after the district
of London in which most of them
lived. It was a long way from the world
of the Charleston, dark lipstick and
skirts above the knee, but that world
too inspired good literature. Scott
Fitzgerald proved it when he wrote
The Great Gatsby, an immediate
reflection of his own social
environment. Dos Passos wrote

Mrs Stewart, head of the Harper's Bazaar office in Paris, is ready for the aeroplane – but emergency unwrapping cannot be considered.

Manhattan Transfer, another milestone in American literature, and the *New Yorker* was launched, two years after *Time Magazine*. Chaplin finished *Gold Rush*, the odd one out in the changing world of Hollywood, now all set for the full exploitation of glamour. As motion pictures became nearer to real life, their influence on fashion increased. Women wanted to imitate the stars' make-up, hairdos and the more wearable of their costumes. Some still dressed in Paris but very talented designers like Adrian were responsible for many innovations and desirable outfits. Their evening gowns even influenced the French couturiers. *Haute couture* in Paris was in full growth. Patou, Lanvin and Vionnet opened boutiques offering a larger public some of their more accessible models and accessories. Chanel issued her famous perfume Number 5 – a master stroke.

The highlight of the year was undoubtedly the exhibition of Decorative Arts. A brand new generation of designers showed the best it had to offer, from glass panels by Lalique to rugs and patchworked clothes designed by Sonia Delaunay – who had painted cars to match. The boyish figures, propeller scarves, ankle chains, cloche hats, long tubular *chemises*, cigarette holders and strings of pearls of the fashionable women fitted into the picture perfectly: they too were *Arts Déco*. Chromed furniture, Cartier jewellery, architecture, glass, mass-produced objects, plastic, concrete – everything was the direct result of the combined influences of Cubism, Diaghilev's *Ballets Russes*, African art, the Bauhaus. Poiret did not want to join in but had the original idea of opening three different establishments on barges moored on the Seine. One was a restaurant, one was for his collections and aboard the third he exhibited the products of his newly founded textile and furnishing firm 'Martine': wall hangings by Dufy, geometric furniture inspired by Cubism and fabrics printed with stylised flowers. The *Arts Déco* style is still with us – and who has forgotten *Tea for Two*?

1926

Chanel's sequinned georgette dress. The top is tied to the dress in a bow. Satin shoes and hardly any jewels.

Neat silk summer suit by Worth with belt passing through the pocket. Diamanté brooches as fancy jewellery.

The mermaid caught in a net: Suzy
Solidor, complete with cork, ankle chain
and rubber shoes.

Fashion had become important to the point of being France's second largest export.

This does not mean, of course, that every woman was able to walk into the best fashion houses to replenish her wardrobe. The couturiers' position was – and remained – equivocal: they needed to keep a degree of exclusivity for their wealthy customers but had also to run their houses as businesses, profitably. On the other hand, the simple lines of their dresses and the small amount of fabric required – two yards might suffice – made them easy to copy. Poiret loathed the situation; Vionnet too, but her architectural method of cutting on the bias was difficult to imitate and would lead any amateur dressmaker into total disaster. Chanel's approach was more objective: "If there is no copying, how are you going to have fashion?" The solution to this problem lay with the ready-to-wear manufacturers. By adapting the original models sold to them by the couturiers and by varying the details of cut and fabric, they ensured that passable imitations of couture clothes could be bought in good shops, large stores or through mail order firms at prices suitable to most budgets. The original impeccably finished silk jersey two-piece suit, worn over a bias-cut silk muslin blouse bought from a Paris house, became the rayon suit of standard size bought off the peg and available to any provincial girl. America was now producing fifty-three million pounds of rayon a year. Only the quality of the accessories would mark the difference. Couturiers could rely on the custom of wealthy women from all over the world. One house had opened a branch in Buenos Aires years before. Women from Rome, Madrid, London, Munich, Vienna, Brussels or the USA attended fashion shows in Paris and placed large orders.

It was the job of fashion magazines to provide detailed reports, not only

56

about *haute couture* but also about its customers – their choice of couturiers, the garments they chose, the personal touches they added and the social gatherings they attended wearing these outfits. All the best fashion publications had a correspondent in Paris. More than a journalist, she would be a woman of good social background, who could easily move within the best society, and who lived in the same style. These periodicals provided the fashion houses with world-wide promotion. It was essential to attract the attention of a world beyond that of the small élite of private clients. To the couturiers, magazines like *Vogue*, *Harper's Bazaar* and *Jardin des Modes* were vital. Nevertheless, one could not always expect smooth dealings between couturiers and magazines. Competition

was fierce, and there were corresponding jealousies and feuds. Vionnet, who had to her credit the most beautiful of evening dresses and was famous for the perfection of every detail of her designs, could not bear Chanel's style and success. She would make such comments as "Oh! Chanel, that *modiste* . . ." Editorial staff got endless complaints: one could not tolerate to share a page with X or bear to see his models reproduced on a page facing Z; why had they allocated so much space to this one and so little to themselves, and so forth. Elna Woodman Chase, former editor of New York *Vogue*, had to put her foot down and make it very clear that her task was to edit the magazine as she wished, independent of pressure from the couturiers. Besides, she remarked, her staff received bagfuls of grumbling

letters while they could scarcely recall a single note of thanks.

Fashion magazines sifted through all the collections and emphasised the very newest lines. The flair and self-confidence they shared with a vanguard of socialites was enough to impose their edicts on the fashion-buying public. They were not averse to liking excesses and eccentricities, but this did not disturb a readership which remained rather snobbish. Indeed, they rarely failed in their prophecies. Such periodicals were not concerned with political issues; their interests were social, cultural and artistic.

In 1926, they reported on the shortest ever hair (women immediately ran to their hairdressers); on the trend to unisex; on women buying men's accessories such as golfing socks or ties. Skirts, they decreed, would be shorter than ever. Maids were set to taking up hems or else the outmoded garments would simply be discarded. With their hair cropped and their cloche hats or turbans worn low on the forehead, attention was naturally drawn to women's eyes. Kohl and mascara started to be used to enlarge them as much as possible, accentuating femininity in an age that seemed otherwise to be moving away from it. In his portraits, Van Dongen has caught perfectly the essence of womanhood in this sophisticated era – sophisticated enough to invade what had hitherto been regarded as male preserves.

This tendency could be interpreted as a sign of liberalisation, but it could apply only superficially. Women enjoyed a great amount of freedom and had no need to liberate themselves from domestic chores, as servants were still plentiful. The war, of course, had given a certain sense of independence to numbers of factory workers who would have otherwise been in service. Still, servants were more difficult to find, please and keep. There were

Moiré patchwork wrapover by Becker.
All the stockings seem to have a ladder.
It was in fact a decorative stitch.

alternatives to domestic work, allowing more private life. British ladies complained in letters to newspapers about the scarcity of domestic labour. They demanded that dole money be refused to women out of work in order to force them back into domestic service. Lady Astor's maid later recalled the difference between the lot of the American and the British servant – the Americans had to work harder but were allowed to stay in bed after late night receptions, had better wages and more time off. Lady Astor might have been American herself, but she was certainly not given to treating her staff with such laxity.

London became paralysed by a general strike that aroused great emotion in the middle and upper classes. In high spirits, young men and undergraduates volunteered to drive buses and to undertake other tasks the workers had abandoned (sometimes slaking their enthusiasm at late night parties instead). Memories of mutinies in the trenches, of communist uprisings abroad and of successive strikes in recent years had a frightening effect on people still protected by the privileges of their class and unwilling for the most part to look at the situation from a point of view other than their own. The strike had hardly begun before troops were sent in. It only lasted nine days, but aggravated the social climate.

In Paris, the Surrealists had decided that society be openly provoked and published their first manifesto. Their aim was to deride values dear to the establishment, to demonstrate the absurdity of an order of things taken for normal and as such, unquestioned. They mocked conventions, indulged in sarcasm, and irritated – with deliberate bad taste – a society which responded beyond all expectations. Any case of apoplexy which resulted directly from their provocations was celebrated with elation. The Surrealists were gifted and intelligent

Ready to go at Chamonix. The woollen cardigan looks inappropriate.

18th century Russian page-boy style over a checked jumper.

– they included Max Ernst, André Breton, Luis Buñuel, Man Ray, Magritte, Eluard, Duchamp. Dali, with his cumbersome paranoia, joined them later. Their heroes were the Marquis de Sade, Gilles de Rais, both conveniently repulsive for the scale and morbidity of their sexual excesses, and the impossibly hermetic writer Raymond Roussel, a wealthy original who on one occasion took his yacht to the Far East, then refused to set foot on shore and left at once. There was also Alfred Jarry, creator of *Père Ubu*. Psychoanalysis, the magic of modern man, was a favourite subject of study. However, as the years passed, respectability settled in and was marked by instances of regrettable pomposity which blunted the sharp blade of their wits. Yet, Surrealism is now acknowledged to have created masterpieces.

Chagall had arrived from Russia, tired of the racial and political limitations imposed by some of the new leaders. Aldous Huxley had seen the last productions of German Expressionism and found them pretentious and melodramatic. D. H. Lawrence wrote *The Plumed Serpent*, T. E. Lawrence *Seven Pillars of Wisdom*. Ramon Novarro was rather splendid in *Ben Hur*, but for millions of women the death of Rudolf Valentino seemed the greatest tragedy ever to occur.

1927

Three dresses by Germaine Lecomte. The left one is very sophisticated in cut; the skirt is cut across with a few pleats and an inset in front. The top has a big cowl neck-line partly stitched up the centre in front to form a ruffle.

The Romans called for bread and circuses. In the late twenties, the flappers and their boy-friends simply wanted more fun – bread was no problem. Night-clubs and cabarets were still enjoying great popularity and a fashionable establishment could take up to £1000 a week.

There was no lack of entertainments, many of them now accessible to all. Much improved cinema techniques allowed spectacular productions such as Cecil B. de Mille's *King of Kings*. Noël Coward had four shows running simultaneously. Adele and Fred Astaire attracted a large public in New York and in London with Gershwin's musical *Lady Be Good*.

Black entertainers had influenced variety shows so much that white artists now became eager to challenge their success, either – like Al Jolson – by adopting similar style and looks, or on the contrary by accentuating differences, as in the *Whitebirds* of Maurice Chevalier and Yvonne Vallée. The impact of black shows had over the years irritated a number of whites, who started to denigrate the blacks, implying their music was in fact of European origin and that they could make precious little claim to originality.

Imaginative ringmasters helped to keep society amused. In London, Cecil Beaton declared 1927 to be the year of a million parties. Mere cocktails were not enough. Call them 'Bosom Caressers' or 'Between the Sheets', by themselves they were now old hat. The new thing was fancy dress parties, as *outré* and extravagant as possible. People came dressed as babies or wearing elaborate masks, all in black or all in white. Glossy magazines devoted page after page to illustrating ideas for costumes, many of them more suitable for a children's carnival. Did the influence come from the superbly original costumes which were seen on stage? Miró, Picasso, Matisse and Braque were designing sets and

Very simple panné velvet dress by Premet, with a sash of gros-grain *and a belt that could not be lower.*

Chanel. The blouse opens on a modestie *sewn underneath as an underyoke. The dress is not meant to unbutton.*

costumes during this year.

In contrast with the oriental explosion of Diaghilev's golden era, new ballets, particularly those staged by Rolf de Maré's Ballets Suedois, were turning to the modern world for inspiration. De Maré's idea was that dance, music, poetry and painting should all be combined together in a resolutely anti-academic way. He favoured the humorous, the mechanistic, the Surrealistic, and he employed Léger, Satie and Picabia. In 1924, one of his ballets called *Relâche* (literally 'closed between shows') had included the projection of René Clair's film *Entracte* ('Interval'). Diaghilev responded by presenting *Le Pas d'Acier*, with constructivist sets and music by Prokofiev, showing scenes inspired by the rhythms of a factory worker's life. This is as far as society would go.

Industry itself was only a theme for a ballet, though the products of industry were there to be enjoyed. Cars were now faster and more comfortable. Some, like the superb Hispano-Suiza, had the lines of a clipper ship. The previous year, Perry Thomas, driving a car of his own design, had broken the world speed record at 172 miles per hour. Aviation was also making great progress. New airports had to be built to cope with international traffic. Pilots could now attempt long distance flights. Lindbergh, who crossed the Atlantic from New York to Paris in thirty-seven hours, remains the most famous of all these pioneers. His daring feat was reported to millions by the radio and the press. Young, modest and good-looking, Lindbergh personified the modern hero. When he landed, he received a delirious welcome.

People were buying more and more wireless sets. What was the news? Stalin had vanquished Trotsky in Russia and the Japanese troops were invading China, already in the grip of civil war. The German economy was

collapsing. Europe had its usual quota of strikes. King George V had received the French president Domergue and had competed at Cowes in the royal yacht *Britannia*. Cowes was one of the peaks of the English season, because the king was always there. In London, where Hartnell had started to establish himself, Chanel opened a boutique.

The place to go to was still the south of France, now invaded by Anglo-Saxons. Cannes was their chief magnet. Many couturiers had opened boutiques there for tourists anxious to keep their tan

all year round and to enjoy gay company in a setting of villas, casinos, beaches and luxury yachts. Biarritz and Deauville were equally elegant, but catered to a different atmosphere. Deauville is not far from Paris, on the Normandy coast, and the casino and the races were its main attractions and people there were very chic. Biarritz was oriented more towards sports. In winter, thanks to this new passion, the ski resort of St Moritz had become an international meeting ground.

1928

Beautiful Vionnet work : cut on the cross, with hand-made ladders. The pleated skirt has hanging points.

Chanel, Deauville summer season. The skirt has exquisite pleating.

St Moritz. Equestrian lower half,
pilot-like bonnet, long scarf and jumper.
The line is perfect.

Neat silhouettes, low hip lines,
evening dresses with bare backs,
pyjamas now worn on the beach, tight
swimsuits, scanty sports clothes, little
dance dresses – all these demanded a
slim body. Losing weight had become
an absolute must: women dieted.
By day, the sheer elegance of Vionnet
or Chanel's simple jerseys were
typical. Beads and pearls embroideries,
chiffons and more obvious touches of
luxury were left to the evenings.
Fashion seemed to have gently settled
on its course, but there were a few
obvious changes. Shingled hair
looked more feminine (while men, as
Cecil Beaton put it, "had for supreme
object to have a head looking like a
wet football"); the waistline was
going up, hems were again going
down a little.
Elsa Schiaparelli, a society lady, born
in Rome nearly forty years before, had
started to be known and now opened
her own fashion house. If any
comparison can be drawn as to the
extent of her influence, it is the names
of Poiret and Chanel which come to
mind: Poiret, because of her close
association with artists who later
brought their individual touches to her
designs and also because, like him, she
once more changed the shape of the
body, restoring the waist and squaring
the shoulders with padding (a line that
was to remain until the end of the
Second World War); Chanel, because
of her use of knits, but in a more
personal way, and keeping strict
lines. Her artistic connections were
with the Cubists and even more
with the Surrealists, with Dali,
Cocteau and later with Christian
Bérard. She launched a range of
hand-knitted jumpers incorporating
trompe d'œuil effects, simulated ruffles.
fake bows or illusory scarves draped
around the hip. She used tweeds for
evening dresses and buttons of all
kinds – there were flowers, guitars,
even edible ones. Aspirins were strung
into necklaces. The bottle for her

64

The triumph of the cloche *(bell, in French). Women have heart-shaped lips and wear mascara. Hats by Le Monnier, Marcelle Lély and Gaby Mono.*

Japanese inspired beach kimono. The shoes are not yet in tune.

perfume 'Shocking' took the shape of Mae West's curvaceous body. Her first private customer had been Anita Loos, the American author of *Gentlemen Prefer Blondes*. Lauren Bacall, Marlene Dietrich and Michèle Morgan were to be among her faithful clients. Schiaparelli had this year included in her collection a culotte reaching just below the knee. It was an appropriate garment for women not yet ready for trousers but committed to many outdoor activities. Chanel, though she knew many artists, did not rely on their talents to inspire her collections. Her strength was to evolve within a constant style. Her least successful models were those which attempted to

please her clients' tastes rather than her own, as in some evening dresses. She did not care much for Schiaparelli "that Italian artist who makes clothes".
If artists' works are a reflection of their environment, the reality of social problems was prominent, logically enough, in countries under stress such as Germany. Bertholt Brecht and Kurt Weil were producing *The Threepenny Opera* and Fritz Lang *Metropolis*. Russian films continued to express the gigantic trauma of the revolution – it was the year of Eisenstein's *October*. In the rest of Europe, the first of a wave of books devoted to the war appeared. It had taken ten years to

distil the nightmare and for the public to recover from the shock.
Hollywood was not yet concerned with such matters. Most producers were a cautious business-minded lot. Very few were willing to consider films as anything other than sheer entertainment. *Our Dancing Daughters*, Joan Crawford's first big success, is typical of this period. The young Mickey Mouse, star of Walt Disney's cartoons, was now appearing in colour.
The bombshell of the year exploded in London, when D. H. Lawrence's *Lady Chatterley's Lover* appeared, expurgated, on the bookstalls.

1929

*This lovely-looking girl wears a shiny waffle-like quilted velvet suit by Chanel,
the blouse and lining fabric are the same. Net fringed bonnet by Le Monnier.*

Winter season at St Moritz. Satin and muslin dress tied in a bow on the side, diamond bracelets and brooch.

Diamonds and precious stones. A clip holds a drape of contrasting colour.

Few people sensed that 1929 was to be the hinge year between the two worst conflagrations in history.

Stalin now held his country in a ruthless grip. He had started the first of his many purges, and had found efficient methods of clearing the political scene of any kind of opposition. People were sent to rot in gaol indefinitely, sent to customary exile in the harsh climate of Siberia or were disposed of by summary execution. Trotsky had lost the struggle. He had to leave Russia and begin the years of exile which ended with his assassination in Mexico.

To most Europeans, Russia was a faraway land, not quite part of Europe, but it was all too close for the neighbouring states which feared for their political independence.

In Italy, the firmly established fascist government was silencing its opponents, often with revolting brutality. Exile abroad or underground activities at home had become the only options left to dissidents. Mussolini wanted to rebuild Italy as a new Roman Empire – hence his enthusiasm for erecting imposing monuments and his taste for colonisation. The notorious Black Shirts led his military parades. Fascist movements were also emerging in other countries such as Spain, Finland and Portugal.

Fascism did not frighten the Western ruling class. They approved of discipline. Englishmen and Frenchmen often condemned what they saw as the leniency of their respective governments in social and industrial matters. They took much the same view about Hitler's mounting influence. There was no cause for anxiety and life went on as usual.

In Great Britain alone, two million telephones had been installed and wireless sets totalled three million. In the USA, the automobile and film industries were among the most dynamic. Plastics and artificial fabrics were also produced on a large scale,

but no one was yet complaining of living in an age of plastic.

Colour was increasingly used in films. Warner Bros even declared they would not make any more black and white features. Kodak introduced the 16mm film, another important improvement, as it made equipment lighter and easier to handle.

The new Hollywood star was Greta Garbo, the Swedish enigma. Her image was distant, remote, inaccessible. Perhaps this explained her durable admirers' emotion, since her acting talents were not exceptional. She had first played in silent films and her first

talkie created suspense: how would her voice sound? Luckily, she was one of those who passed the test. *A Woman of Affairs* established her as one of the top world motion-picture stars. She was in a class of her own, quite impossible to challenge. Copying her style would have been pointless, and it was not attempted. Her rivals aimed for sex appeal, not mystery.

Garbo wore her hair waved and nearly shoulder length, a personal choice but one in tune with a tendency towards a more feminine look. Bosoms discreetly reappeared, this time as nature made them, not turned into a single bulky

67

Left: *Mistinguett and suitors in knickerbockers. She wears a three-layered dress by Louiseboulanger.*

Mistinguett, the French sex symbol . . . was it all in the mind of the beholders? Overt sexiness meant naughtiness. She wears a woollen jersey swimming suit.

This suit is less tight but much more suggestive.

uplifted shape. Women were adopting a more natural shape. From now on, fashion evolved without submitting the body to changes so radical as to forcibly transform the whole anatomy. With women now wearing tight jersey swimming suits and shorts (the latter first appeared in the USA), this was only logical.

The rhythm of life was less frenetic and so fashion for a while became softer. Cloche hats had looked like pilots' helmets; long jackets, floating scarves and loosely tied bows brought a new suppleness. Evening dresses, short in front, dipped into trains at the back. Sandals were considered elegant and so were berets, preferably worn at seaside resorts. Schiaparelli's patterned jumpers in a variety of geometric designs were copied everywhere. They were an echo of Mondrian's totally abstract canvases. The Museum of Modern Art opened in New York with a large exhibition of Impressionists. Modern art was at last

being officially recognised, but its real supporters were still a tiny minority. On the literary front, two outstanding books about the 1914–18 war were published – the German Erich Maria Remarque's *All Quiet on the Western Front*, and Hemingway's *Farewell to Arms*. The first was made into a film the following year. The general conviction was that such a holocaust could never happen again. Yet, the titles chosen by other writers now sound awkwardly tuned to the

69

Two similar geometrically patterned
jumpers and finely pleated printed
skirts. On the right, by Patou.

Paquin at Biarritz. Belted patterned
jumper with diamanté clip, quilted
borders and beret.

imminent future: Cocteau's *Les
Enfants Terribles*, one of his most
interesting books, with Surrealistic
undertones; Noël Coward's *Bitter
Sweet*; and Faulkner's *The Sound and
the Fury*.

The sudden collapse of Wall Street,
the centre of the American Stock
Exchange, took the world by surprise.
It was like the volcanic eruption which
engulfed Pompeii. Fortunes were
reduced to ashes overnight, panic was
complete and misery struck millions of

Hats by Charlotte, Jenny, Gaby Mono and Patou, inspired by the pilots' helmets. The brows are plucked and realigned.

people all over the Western hemisphere. The wealthy, those who did not earn wages, but who lived on the interest from investments, saw their income shrink catastrophically. Only real estate remained a reliable basis for wealth. Numerous businesses had to close, or at the very best slow down their production considerably. The immediate consequence was massive unemployment and subsequent destitution for the masses.

In Europe, the situation was hardly better than it was in America. American loans ceased and the volume of exports to America fell sharply. Yet, there were enough survivors able to maintain, if only at a reduced scale, their accustomed standards of life. The Empire State Building, a monument to American enterprise, was begun that year. But the joyous spirit of the twenties, its carefree irresponsibility, died with the decade. It was like the end of an old-fashioned moral tale.

At the time, the crash was seen as a kind of conclusion. To us now, it looks more like a sour beginning. Before the war, wealth had been solid, immutable; the rich believed they would always be rich. But from the very beginning of the post-war period, doubt began to creep in. Some people were ruined by the revolution in Russia, others by the German inflation. Much of the money in the twenties was new money, made by frantic speculation.

Intellectually at least, most people remained confident that the boom would last, but deep in their hearts, there was a seed of doubt. It was this, as much as the dark memories of the war, that had given so many of them an appetite for amusement which could never be quenched.

1930

Chiffon dress by Paquin with long-sleeved bolero. The lower half of the dress is cut on the cross.

Very simple looking dress by Chanel with yoke and shoulder piece cut as a short cape and diamanté buckle.

The radiant Josephine Baker with Paul
Derval, director of the Folies-Bergère, at
Deauville. Dress by Drecoll Beer. The
jacket has asymmetrical fur trimming.

There have been many theories about
the trends and moods of the fashion
world. As can be expected, they differ
tremendously. Art can be absorbed
simply as sensation or, on the contrary,
it can be dissected like an insect.
There are experts who find it difficult
to accept beauty other than as the
result of calculated thinking – theory is
responsible for everything – the last
brush-stroke, the last minimal dot of
red.

One theory about fashion is that hems
go down in line with the economy. In
1930, they plunged. Patou presented
his new collection to an assembly of
elegant women but dared not be
present. He awaited their reactions:
all his models had much longer skirts.
When his assistant rushed backstage
to report that all the clients sitting
there were pulling at their skirts, he
knew he had won. They already felt
démodées. Chanel had to follow
Patou's lead, for once losing to her arch
rival. It did not mean that Patou was
the most avant-garde couturier, but
simply that he had rightly sensed a
change of mood. As a result of the
slump, fashion houses were showing
only a quarter of their usual number
of models – only 100 per collection.
But dresses now required more fabric
than the two yards which had once
been sufficient. Chanel's jerseys were
now so popular that she designed
garments for foreign stores and had
opened a factory employing 2500
people.

High life was less spectacular, but it
was still lively in spite of a few
casualties – those who had disappeared
from the ranks into bankruptcy. As the
crisis made itself felt, political topics
began to be discussed in fashion
magazines along with the usual
features on clothes and social events.
Mrs Simpson, an American resident in
England, attracted attention for her
strict and impeccable elegance.
At the other end of the social scale,
millions were living on the dole. In

205

73

Left: *Mrs Martinez de Hoz, a woman of superb and unfailing elegance who often dressed at Vionnet's.*

Fête de l'Elégance *at the* Polo de Bagatelle *in June. Lots of printed chiffon and long dresses.*

England, marchers in their thousands, mainly from the north, took the road to London in a desperate attempt to attract public and government attention to their misery. There were many clashes with the police. Some men marched into the Ritz, disturbing the elegant set sipping tea – a striking contrast immediately reported in the papers.

Many of the young men who had volunteered during the general strike four years before were now in sympathy with the helpless workers. Politics entered everyone's life and individual political inclinations took on a new importance, even in ordinary social intercourse.

The King of England had recovered from a near-fatal illness and the British Government was trying to find a way of dealing with India's independence movement. This was inspired by Gandhi, a diminutive and

dedicated man who had great influence with the Indian people. He rejected the use of violence and instead launched a civil disobedience campaign.

The Western countries had a flourishing literary life, with Evelyn Waugh, Aldous Huxley, the two Lawrences, Noël Coward, Somerset Maugham, W. H. Auden, T. S. Eliot, Bernard Shaw, Virginia Woolf, all at work in England. Giraudoux, St Exupéry, Claudel, Gide and Cocteau were writing in France, where Proust was also being posthumously discovered. America now had a generation of writers who wholly identified with their country: Sinclair Lewis, Dos Passos, Eugene O'Neill, Upton Sinclair, William Faulkner. Fitzgerald and Hemingway were among the few who set their stories in Europe.

The cinema was entering a golden age

and flourished if only because it helped people to forget the hard times they were enduring. With the music hall (which it would soon kill off), it was the most popular form of entertainment. Gary Cooper, who had begun his career in silent movies in 1927, now appeared in many feature films, usually as the handsome young man who could do no wrong. His new type of hero contrasted sharply with the irresistible seducers Valentino and Novarro had played before him. Homespun charm had replaced Latin sensuality; cowboy gear triumphed over exotic burnous. One of Cooper's films was *Morocco*, with Marlene Dietrich, who shared with Garbo a guttural accent and high cheekbones. Marlene was perfect as the heartless *femme fatale* and she had superb legs. She knew how to get the best out of her looks, and could even give the studio specialists a few tips on

Satin evening pyjamas by Vionnet, finely stitched and pleated, but difficult to wear.

Linen trousers by Rochas with twenty rows of stitches at the bottom. A model 're-invented' much later.

Tweed dress and 7/8ths jacket with matching hat by Jenny.

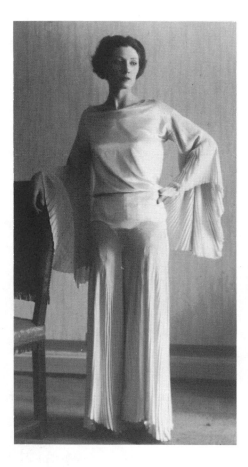

make-up. She accentuated her features by plucking her eyebrows, a fashion soon to be widely adopted. Her smash hit was the German *Blue Angel*, directed by Sternberg, who masterminded her early career. Among the many emigrants who worked in Hollywood was Alfred Hitchcock, whose film *Murder* showed his quality as a master of suspense. In complete contrast were the anarchic Marx Brothers. *Animal Crackers* demonstrated their gift for the comedy of the absurd.

People were by now better informed. Newsreels and broadcasts had widened their horizons. In Great Britain, youth hostels were founded: young people felt a need to discover the world and the hostels enabled them to do it cheaply. Entertainment was organised to reach the greatest possible number. 1930 was also the year of the first World Football Cup.

Increased internationalism contrasted with a sharpening of the class conflict. Labour agitation flared everywhere, and sometimes it won important victories. Despite the slump, working conditions did improve, though working people remained disenchanted with their respective governments because of their inability to improve the economy. Spain was in the news, as the throne of King Alfonso was shaken by violent factions from both Left and Right. Both Mussolini and Hitler were growing in confidence and reputation, and they now denounced the Treaty of Versailles. In many countries, authoritarian monarchy had long been accepted, but civilian dictatorships were as yet a new political concept. The implication of such régimes was not as yet fully understood. People were impressed by Mussolini's propaganda: they thought he had restored the Italian economy

and had given Italy a new spirit of discipline, and they believed Hitler could do the same for Germany. Foreigners scarcely noticed fascism's harsh repression of all internal criticism and overlooked its scant respect for civil liberties. Even the working classes were sometimes tempted by the promises of the radical right. And where the Western democratic governments were concerned, communism remained their chief bogey, thanks to its identification with the abhorred Bolshevik régime in Russia. Because the privileges of the ruling class were challenged by the communists rather than by the fascists, many politicians chose to worry about the Reds and failed to appreciate the realities of fascism.

1931

Healthy looking Miss Europe, sporting a navy and white jersey outfit by Heim at Biarritz.

Lanvin jersey outfit and pearls for the sophisticated Deauville sea-side resort.

The slump continued. Concern with fashion began to seem irrelevant. Rich households were run on a reduced staff, and society entertaining became increasingly informal. Clothes followed suit: jumpers were worn even in the late afternoon.

The American Mainbocher – who was, with Schiaparelli, Mrs Simpson's favourite couturier – valiantly opened a new fashion house in Paris, after a spell as editor of *Vogue*. There were other foreigners in French *haute couture*, who could not have hoped to win the same recognition outside Paris. Piguet was Swiss, Maggy Rouff came from Belgium, Schiaparelli was Italian.

Fashion houses were trying hard to adjust to economic pressures. Chanel produced a range of evening dresses made of cotton, a much cheaper innovation. It was no longer smart to look smart. The overall impression was one of restraint: tailored suits, little hats, tight jackets – everything had a skimped look. Extravagant flights of the imagination were out, together with other kinds of excess. There was a deep divide between the glamour of Hollywood – the luxury of its silky outfits that ravished the cinema-going masses – and the down-to-earth allure of *haute couture*. Jean Harlow was in the ascendant, a platinum blonde star who acted out fantasies remote from the grim reality of daily life. Hollywood was the only place, it seemed, where luxury was still at home. Otherwise, artificial fabrics, zips and paper patterns helped to bring down the cost of fashion. False eyelashes were available by now, but had to be applied by skilled beauticians. Nail varnish, lipstick and other cosmetics, now to be found in all the big chain stores, helped to make women feel they were coming one step nearer to their favourite screen stars. The spectacular side of prohibition had caught the imagination of the producers. The first 'tough guy'

Summer culotte-suit by Heim.

Biarritz in September, straight out of a film set. The men have heavily brilliantined hair.

gangster films appeared, with James Cagney as 'chief heavy'. Chaplin released *City Lights*; *Frankenstein* marked the return of another, more gothic, kind of fantasy. Technological advance was one of the few things that boosted the popular morale. Captain Campbell drove *Bluebird* at 246 mph – a land speed record. An Italian pilot reached 246 mph in the air, while Professor Piccard's balloon ascended to a height of ten miles above the earth. The first air mail arrived from Australia and air mail letter boxes appeared on the streets of London.

The monarchy had collapsed in Spain and there was now a republic. In Germany, where the economic situation was so bad that the banks closed their doors for nearly a month, Hitler was gaining support from a growing number of industrial

magnates. The post-war republics of Central Europe were in scarcely better shape economically. Here too, fascist parties were gaining strength.

In England, Oswald Mosley had just founded the British Union of Fascists, popularly known as the Black Shirts. England had an external debt of £100 million sterling and no reasons to hope for a rapid recovery. The King even offered to cut £50,000 a year from his civil list.

Gandhi continued to create trouble and spent some time in gaol before he was allowed out to meet the King-Emperor in London, but the meeting led nowhere: Gandhi was determined to continue his campaign for Indian independence. The hard-hit Lancashire cotton industry suffered from the troubles in India, the chief source of raw material.

Most countries felt vulnerable. King

George V received the German Chancellor as a gesture of friendship and people were organising peace demonstrations. People wanted peace – at nearly any price – to stay, but they felt their world was collapsing and the tensions created by political and economic uncertainties were hard for them to bear.

Comfortable sports coat by Marcel Rochas with pocket flaps. It would be just as smart today.

This neat line is more typical of the thirties, in its sober classicism.

Roosevelt was elected President of a country which now had nearly fourteen million unemployed. In such a context, one could have expected fashion to inspire only moderate interest, even among the wealthiest and most mindless of women. But the economic situation was not wholly to the disadvantage of the American fashion industry. What the war had not achieved, the crash did: American buyers had withdrawn from Paris. For the American designers, it was a unique opportunity. The fashion magazines had to pay more attention to what they were doing. The time was ripe for good ready-to-wear manufacturers to increase their prestige among elegant customers. Charles James was one of the best stylists and his influence was soon felt. Hollywood continued to provide fodder for dreams with the help of Adrian's striking outfits. Garbo was seen wearing a man's evening suit. The idea was thought shocking at the time but was soon afterwards adopted by the more daring.

It was to be another good year for films: Marlene Dietrich appeared in *Shanghai Express*, James Cagney played another gangster in *Scarface*, Gary Cooper starred in *Farewell to Arms*, based on Hemingway's novel, and Shirley Temple, groomed as a doll, made her début and immediately became the public's darling. She had pretty curls, pretty smiles and could even tap dance. A number of other child actors were fiercely competing for stardom – or was it their parents? Shirley was a big box office success only in her childhood years, whereas Judy Garland, Mickey Rooney and later Elizabeth Taylor managed to retain their fame into adulthood. The first *Tarzan* movie was shown – could he be considered as Hollywood's response to a taste for athletics? It was the turn of Los Angeles to play host to the Olympic Games. Very different from the first *Tarzan* was *Night After*

Rosie, one of the Dolly Sisters, wearing a five-tone Molyneux evening dress and lots of diamonds.

Night. The star of the film was Mae West. With a seemingly out-of-fashion curvy figure, a very personal way of undulating rather than walking, and a complete command of the *double entendre*, she immediately became very popular. She might have taken her part very seriously, but she always seemed to wink at the audiences in a manner suggesting that it could be lots of fun being a sex object, and the audiences loved it. The most scandalous film of the year was *Extase*, in which Hedy Lamarr briefly appeared in the nude. Well over a hundred films were produced in the year and many of them were later released in most Western countries.

Russia had cut itself out of such entertainment. Stalin was now firmly in charge. His methods were brutal in a way pre-revolutionary rulers would not have found surprising. Yet another dictatorship had been founded, but this time in the name of the people's betterment and future happiness. Many eminent Russian artists were banned as decadent, Rachmaninoff among them. Russia needed all its might to restore the country's economy and Stalin was determined to make his country one of the great twentieth-century industrial powers. There were many problems, and a serious state of famine.

Censorship was definitely in the air: Hitler, whose Nazi party had won a large number of seats in the Reichstag in the recent elections, had also his choice of 'decadents', who were now living in insecurity. His list of undesirables was not always very different from Stalin's. It included all non-Aryans – Jews in particular, but also gypsies – all non-Nazis, all homosexuals and all artists who did not conform to the party line. Many of the prescribed were trying to leave Germany; they knew it could not be long before Hitler achieved power. Hitler had not yet reached his ultimate ambition. Communists and

Subtle effect of chevron stripes with small diamanté clip.

Very classical, this is the perfect example of the 'little dress' that goes anywhere. By Redfern.

other parties were still blocking his way to power, but by means of violence, propaganda and intimidation, he was flattening any opposition to his goal of absolute power. There were frequent clashes in the streets of Berlin between his Brown Shirts and members of left-wing groups. There were over five and a half million unemployed in Germany. Hitler made inflamed speeches, had a propaganda machine imposingly orchestrated by Goebbels and he aroused massive enthusiasm. He controlled huge numbers of disciplined and loyal followers from all walks of life. The accent was on work, on a healthy discipline and on total devotion to Fatherland and Führer. Despite the emphasis on order, Hitler's forces took more and more liberties with legality: raids, beatings and other similar

incidents became common and there was nothing the government could or would do about them. One can see how Hitler's programme could present a tempting solution to a nation deeply discouraged, crippled by appalling economic problems. What was wrong with work, open-air activities, songs around the camp fire and love of one's land? Nothing indeed, except that intolerance leading to forceful suppression of free expression, extreme racialism – either the fruit of an unbalanced mind or a vile expedient to channel people's frustrations on to a scapegoat – and an all-powerful military system are the basic tools of a totalitarian régime.

Hitler did not lack admirers and allies abroad. Portugal was now ruled by Salazar and his régime had fascist overtones. Here too, economic collapse had let in dictatorship. England's situation was not improving. Hunger marches, better organised, continued to fill the roads. Unemployment was not only hitting blue-collar workers. There were now nearly three million out of work in Great Britain and it was said that men with degrees were two a penny. Even the rich were now feeling the pinch.

In Paris, couturiers drastically cut their prices. Dresses had tight busts not requiring much corsetry, higher collars or round white ones, called *col Claudine* after Colette's schoolgirl heroine. Berets were worn sideways and there were sailor hats. Striped fabrics assembled in a variety of patterns were in fashion. Following Schiaparelli's lead, sleeves were given great emphasis. They were the most striking feature of the collections, puffed or leg-of-lamb-shaped. Evening dresses still had bare backs. A new-comer, Alix, afterwards known as Grès, opened her own house. She had started her career as a sculptress, a training that was to influence all her designs. She draped soft jerseys directly on the model without

preliminary design or patterns. The effect was classical, almost architectural. Her style was very individual and immediately appealed to elegant women.

Haute couture had lost a great deal of its frivolity, but the fashionable still had to be fashionable. It was an absolute part of life and there was no question of stepping out and brandishing the flag of independence, any more than of going out without a hat or gloves. One was gauged by one's clothing. It was a sign of class allegiance far more than it is today.

Yet, fashion had changed tremendously since the beginning of the century – only thirty years previously. The superb deportment of the previous generation had vanished. Women's carefree attitudes had given place to a self-conscious awareness. There was more reserve. The old standards of life were no longer taken for granted. News that could have been ignored before was now brought into everyone's home by the radio. The most sensational story of the year was the kidnapping of baby Lindbergh, son of the American pilot and national hero.

The best writers bore witness to the troubles of the time and gave a more balanced view than newspapers. The extreme situation made middle-class men like George Orwell look both profoundly and passionately at the conditions endured by members of the working class. The literature of social concern was to dominate the thirties.

The white bow hides the collar and the jacket opens on to the blouse. By Chanel.

Patou designed this jersey suit. The jacket has four pockets and buttons stop at the waist.

Mrs Heim wears this coat with double
lapel and big pinched cuffs lined with the
same fabric.

Fashion was feeling the pinch more than ever. In the course of five years, the *haute couture* industry had slipped from second to twenty-seventh place in the French exports table. American buyers at least were starting to come back in small numbers, but England, following a 'Buy British' campaign, was patronising its own fashion houses. Victor Stiebel had opened the previous year. There were also Digby Morton and the established Molyneux, Hartnell, Creed, Worth and Rahvis. Although Paris remained the capital of *haute couture*, much that she had to offer could now also be found abroad. Of course, one could always expect something new from France – it came mainly from Schiaparelli, who continued to experiment with sleeves. The newest shape was a square heavily padded shoulder-line.

Hollywood still had good reasons to promote dreams and abandon restraint. If the basic shape of women originated in France, Hollywood imposed the universal idea of beauty. Women were wearing bright lipstick and eye-shadow, artificial effects in contrast with the severity of their clothes, but then, women always succeed in tipping the balance in favour of femininity. Hair was a little longer, curled, topped with a beret. The waist was more accentuated. Women wore practical outfits but they were also aiming at the way Garbo looked in the most romantic scenes of *Queen Christina*. Clothes were more subdued than ever, but artificial fabrics, cellophane, sequins, etc., permitted a touch of frivolity. There were distractions such as *King Kong* or *She Done Him Wrong*, starring Mae West and the unknown Cary Grant, whom she had chosen herself, but politics were yet again eclipsing everything else, even though Mussolini once warned Hitler that whatever he wanted to impose, fashion was the greatest dictator of all. It was Hitler's year. Roosevelt's

phrase from his inauguration speech, "The only thing we have to fear is fear itself", was all too timely. Hitler indeed wasted no time. As soon as he was appointed Chancellor, he hastened into action. The Reichstag was burned down. This supplied a good pretext to blame the opposition and at the same time to suspend civil liberties and the freedom of the press. Hitler's racial hatred could now be officially satisfied: Jewish businesses and professions were boycotted throughout the country. The more dynamic and

affluent Jews fled into exile. When Louis XIV persecuted the Protestants in the seventeenth century, this deprived his country of a valuable number of skilled and educated men whose brains and industry benefited their host countries. The same thing happened in Germany. Scientists, musicians, intellectuals and artists, not all of them Jewish, emigrated, to contribute their talents to the enrichment of other cultures. Kandinsky and Paul Klee left Germany and so did Fritz Lang,

Schiaparelli models her own creations – the accordion pleated square sleeves are levelled with the bolero.

who later continued his career in Hollywood. Lang's last German film, *The Testament of Dr Mabuse*, was more than the Nazis would tolerate. His wife, the *cinéaste* Leni Reifenstahl, remained in Germany, a convinced admirer of the régime. Later in the year, Hitler was granted dictatorial powers, to run until 1937. He suppressed the trade unions. The way was now clear. In new elections, a subdued population gave the Nazis ninety-two per cent of its votes. Many Jews wanted to emigrate to Palestine, where for years Jewish settlement had been a matter of great controversy. Officially, the country was under British control. Frightened at the idea that a sudden influx of immigrants would cause violent clashes with the Arabs, the quota of immigrants was strictly limited. The Jews also faced difficulties when they wished to settle elsewhere. Thanks to the Nazi contagion, anti-semitism was rampant in Europe. England had Mosley; France had a mixture of royalists and right-wingers ready to swear that all ills were the fruits of Machiavellian Jewish conspiracies. The Dreyfus affair had split France at the beginning of the century and was still vivid in memory. Anti-semitism was matched by anti-clericalism. The French left was traditionally anti-clerical.

Now the new Spanish republic nationalised Church property and closed Church schools. A portion of the population was dreading the disappearance of the old order, when Church and State had been firmly allied. The supporters of established religion preferred to rally the cause of fascism in Spain as they did elsewhere.

1934

Arletty wears a diaphanous hat by Talbot at the Compétition d'Elégance Automobile. *She starred in many films by Carné.*

Why should politics play so large a part in a book about fashion? Because fashion is inseparably part of history. When garments were entirely hand-sewn, in pre-industrial times, fashion took decades rather than years to evolve. There was in any case a fixed division between the peasantry who wore clothes which changed hardly at all and the upper and middle classes who, as we know from their portraits, did respond to the dictates of fashion. But it was only after the French revolution of 1799 that women's looks changed dramatically almost from year to year. During the nineteenth century, industry drew into towns factory workers in their thousands and the mass-produced garments made most working women look alike. The war of 1914–1918 was another turning point, as the technology it engendered produced improvements of benefit to all. However strongly class differences remained, the sartorial gap between an upper-class woman and a factory worker had greatly diminished, as everyone was subject, though in varying degrees, to the same fluctuations and even shared the same tastes. Technology brought an element of democracy into society, as its most characteristic products were worth marketing only if mass produced. Fashion as an industry welcomed frequent changes in style, as these stimulated sales.

In 1934, elegant women were opting for a very neat, strict look. Popular fashions were even more influenced by Hollywood ideals: make-up was more obvious and behaviour more sexually overt.

Outdoor life was now very much the thing and the boldest went to nudist camps. Young city dwellers took to cycling and camping wearing their shorts and home-made jumpers. The wealthier remained faithful to beach pyjamas, flared trousers and wrapped-over gowns. Two-piece bathing suits were occasionally seen and Jacques Heim was one of their best designers.

In townwear, the few innovations were largely Schiaparelli's: she made box jackets, gathered at the neck, which were worn short over a simple dress. The waist was slightly higher so as to follow the line of the jacket. Bonnets were in and cumbersome sleeves were still fashionable, if not particularly becoming. Schiaparelli decided to emphasise lapels and to give them a winged effect. The strictness of her line was difficult to wear but superbly elegant when worn successfully.

Exceptionally, it was in London that a couturier's name was this year on everyone's lips. Princess Marina of Greece was marrying the Duke of Kent. Well known to the British public, her charm and cheerful personality made her very popular. She chose Molyneux for her trousseau and the detailed designs were shown in

The best of British elegance. Signed Worth.

Rather flat hats. The brim is variously wide. Leg of mutton sleeves by G. Lecomte, hats by Rose Valois.

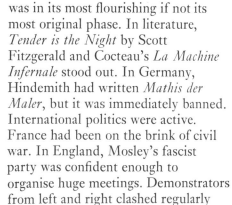

Vogue. Molyneux gained added prestige and the magazines were well pleased.

Fashion news was in short supply, and there was little innovation in the arts. Not that artists had disappeared – individual creators such as Honegger, Stravinsky and Picasso were producing new works – but the arts in general were at a standstill. Giacometti was becoming better known and Calder, with his stabiles and mobiles, had something new to offer. Surrealism was in its most flourishing if not its most original phase. In literature, *Tender is the Night* by Scott Fitzgerald and Cocteau's *La Machine Infernale* stood out. In Germany, Hindemith had written *Mathis der Maler*, but it was immediately banned. International politics were active. France had been on the brink of civil war. In England, Mosley's fascist party was confident enough to organise huge meetings. Demonstrators from left and right clashed regularly in London. Belgium had prohibited all uniformed rallies in an attempt to suppress the paramilitary factions now active everywhere else. While hostilities between the European Right and Left were escalating, the USSR was busy signing trade pacts, most notably with England and with the USA. The Russians badly needed wheat and tools while the West, though reluctant to deal with the Bolsheviks, needed foreign exports and preferred to think of Russia on their

Dress Agnès Drecoll with bouquet of real orchids. Only for a perfect figure. Hat by Talbot.

Mr and Mrs Buster Keaton in Deauville, still unsmiling and not especially fashion-conscious.

side. It was now obvious that Hitler's aggression might not confine itself to Germany. His latest move had been to liquidate his differences with Roehm and his Brown Shirts in a night of mass murder. The Saar was returned to Germany and its steel factories would now be making arms instead of domestic appliances. The British increased the RAF budget as Churchill warned of a potential German air menace.

Behind the scenes, scientists had achieved major results in their researches. Neutrons, protons, atoms figured in their reports. These marked a substantial advance into the sensations of the atomic era. The Joliot-Curies, husband and wife, discovered radioactivity.

Politicians already knew that another war was a possibility. Yet, people wanted peace, on their own terms. They reacted to the menace they vaguely sensed, not by compromise but by taking extreme stands to match what they regarded as extreme situations. The democratic governments had to buy time. Their countries were not yet strong enough to embark on a plan of intensified rearmament. Besides, there were still hopes of saving peace, even at a price.

1935

This lamé evening dress seems rather
inspired by Hollywood – more sexy than
just elegant.

Satin evening dress by Lelong, more
classical than glamorous

Haute couture was in need of inspiration. Despite a tendency towards less severity, the ruling couturiers were not inclined to radical change. The timing would not have been right and besides, women were now more careful, preferring to alter some of their outfits rather than to buy too many new ones. On one hand, there was the military look: square shoulders, breast pockets, belts, berets, sports shoes; and on the other, more suppleness, flounces or accordion-pleated skirts, soft ample sleeves gathered at the cuffs. People longed for a little more frivolity. Evening dresses were much influenced by Hollywood, naturally enough, as these were the most elaborate items in most women's wardrobes. Otherwise, the prevailing strictness of style imposed its limitations, which it was difficult to overcome. Fashion houses determined to concentrate on refined detail, and presented collections full of dresses of imaginative and sophisticated cut. Schiaparelli opened her boutique as the Popular Front was being formed in France. The latter was a hasty union of left-wing parties attempting to restore a national balance threatened by chaos. The situation was not particularly welcomed by the upper classes, as they had hoped the darkest hours of the slump were over. They would have liked to forget their troubles and sail away to New York aboard the brand new *Normandie*.

In the USA, Mr Roosevelt was concentrating on improving the nation's economy. Millions of Americans nevertheless continued to survive in hardship and misery. It was the turn of the country dwellers to suffer as much or even more than the urban masses, for America was suffering from the elements. In some areas, not a drop of rain had relieved the endless miles of parched earth scorched by dust storms. Insects were devouring the remaining crops. Wells dried up. Two-thirds of the country

Very wide cuffless sleeves and scarf. The dress is cut on the cross and slit at the hem. Mainbocher.

Astrakhan-trimmed suit by Nina Ricci with simulated pockets and a breast-plate collar.

Winter dress by Piguet with short cape and matching muff. The very wide belt will come back in the fifties.

was affected and thousands of small farmers bundled their families and possessions on to battered cars and took to the road in a desperate and aimless exodus. So many states were affected that relief, help and shelter were hard to find.

Jazz had evolved. The new thing was swing – light, humorous, up tempo. None played it better than Fats Waller. His music was fun, and so were Busby Berkeley's films. Great tap dancing there, clever tricks, ingenious choreography, with a multitude of dancers dressed like flowers, displayed on revolving staircases or around dozens of white pianos which were reflected in as many mirrors – a true musical kaleidoscope. The latest, *Gold Diggers*, had Ginger Rogers in the leading part.

The British mostly preferred to stay at

home for the Silver Jubilee of King George V. The sovereign and Queen Mary were busy visiting all parts of their kingdom. They received delegations from all corners of the world and the people were celebrating with bunting, bands, parties, and military parades. Crowds rallied at Buckingham Palace shouting "We want George!" The monarchy had never been so popular. Simple, full of concern for his people, George V was the kind of father figure his subjects wanted. However, the King's health prevented him from attending some of the ceremonies held in his honour. He had been the first British monarch to address the nation on the radio, but his Christmas broadcast this year was to be his last. But the Prince of Wales, who enjoyed the pleasures of society life, was also popular, although

rumours of his association with Mrs Simpson did not please people in court circles.

The dictators were still restless. Mussolini realised his dreams of conquest by invading Abyssinia while Hitler had now outlawed the Jews and imposed the Swastika as the official flag. His people could enjoy his presence in their homes thanks to television. It was proving another useful development in the service of propaganda.

Britain was not yet able to benefit from this innovation, but thanks to the brilliant thinking of the publisher Allen Lane, it could now afford to read more books for less money – Penguin paperbacks had made their début – a quiet revolution in the world of publishing.

Simple, chic dress by Maggy Rouff with just two clips and a few buttons at the sleeves. Hat by Reboux.

This outfit by Alix takes a bit of self-confidence. Hat and jacket in black monkey and satin skirt.

The dreaded Popular Front now governed France. Though worried businessmen despatched their capital to foreign banks, socialism did not finish them off.

Fashion, under the circumstances, reacted bravely. It was, after all, bound to be the first victim of economic and political fluctuations. *Vogue* put the words '*Vive le Front plissé populaire!*' under a picture of a cheerful model wearing a blouse with a pleated front. The couturiers defied austerity with an explosion of colour. Schiaparelli launched Shocking Pink, an outrageous fuchsia red that would have been thought the lowest of taste a few years earlier. But now good taste no longer meant an airy reserve and neutral tweeds to go with it. Hollywood had seen to that. Ostentation was still out, but dash was in: make-up combining reds, crimsons, browns, greens and purples; tailored suits, which, with their skimped skirts and boxy jackets, often seemed to be the result of a random choice made among disparate outfits.

Designers felt they had to restrict daytime fantasy to hats, and sheer luxury was reserved for evening wear, in reaction against the limitations of what was worn during the day. Glittering lamés and sequins were popular. Women wore crinolines inspired by a romantic Hollywood version of the Victorian era.

Ten years after their début in Paris, the Surrealists held their first exhibition in London, while Hitler put on a show of 'degenerate art', which contained many modern masterpieces. It created public interest of a kind the Nazis had hardly counted on and was promptly closed.

Germany was busy. It was her turn to be host to the Olympic Games, immortalised by Jesse Owens' performances and by Leni Reifenstahl's film. The Nazis were developing their armament industry, and they gave support to Franco, a

Hats by Colette Clauday, Line Borel and Schiaparelli. Soft looks and square shoulders.

rebel Spanish general who was leading his supporters and his Moroccan troops in an armed insurrection against the Republic.

The Spanish civil war had begun in earnest and the whole of Europe was moved by the conflict. This was not just a struggle for power but a bitter war of ideals. Everywhere, both the Right and Left saw the war as profoundly symbolic. Outsiders flocked to take part. Intellectuals and unemployed workers rallied to the Republicans under the various banners of Socialism, Communism, Trotskyism and Anarchism. Mussolini and Hitler sent more than men. Spain gave them a unique opportunity to test their modern weaponry. Malraux, in his novel *L'Espoir*, and Picasso with *Guernica* – exhibited in 1937 at the Paris World Fair – indignantly recorded its efficiency. Great Britain, disapproving of both sides, refused to become involved, and persuaded twenty-seven other governments – surprisingly the French socialist régime among them – into adopting a policy of non-intervention. Nobody really wanted to provoke Italy and Germany at this point, even indirectly.

Edward VIII, despite some popular support for his cause, preferred to renounce the throne rather than Mrs Simpson. The King, as head of the Church of England, could not marry a twice divorced woman. He was succeeded by his younger brother, the Duke of York, who took the name George VI. The King, his wife Elizabeth, and their two young daughters, Elizabeth and Margaret, were a happy family. The nation took the new monarch to its heart. Edward, now the Duke of Windsor, went into exile, in France, where at long last he married his American divorcée. Her trousseau had been designed by Mainbocher and photographs of the event were flashed round the world.

1938

Knickerbockers and safari jacket by Freddy,
elastic belt, permanent wave and cotton gloves.

Television was introduced in England and nylon stockings appeared in the shops.

In Paris, in the world of fashion, it was the turn of Jean Dessès and of the young Spaniard Balenciaga – Spain was decidedly not the place for a couturier just then. Hartnell was enjoying renewed prestige: his success with the Duchess of Gloucester's wedding dress attracted the patronage of other members of the royal family. Errol Flynn cut a dash in *The Charge of the Light Brigade*, Disney ravished everyone with *Snow White* and *Modern Times* starred Chaplin and his wife Paulette Goddard – but Chaplin's sarcasm made some people wince. Easier to take was Hitchcock's *The Lady Vanishes*.

There was a jolly new dance – the Lambeth Walk; there was Benny Goodman's music; the New York Fair; and there was a big novel by the unknown Margaret Mitchell. It was called *Gone with the Wind* and quickly became a runaway bestseller.

Times seemed to be better. Women like Lady Mendl could still give enormous parties. She had three plane-loads of roses flown from London to Paris and entertained her guests with three orchestras and a circus show. Some of Vionnet's dresses still cost only £20. And the new English King paid a state visit to Paris.

If only the year could have continued on the same note. But, despite a renewal of gaiety, the international situation became worse. It was all faithfully recorded in the pages of the newly founded *Picture Post*. German troops had entered Austria. Most people still clung to the hope that Hitler's ambitions were limited to the Anschluss he had now brought about. Hitler was pleased with Mussolini's refusal to intervene and sent him a telegram: "Mussolini, I shall never forget this." Libya, meanwhile, was declared Italian, following Abyssinia

Very pre-war hair style to which Simone de Beauvoir has remained faithful. Beach outfit by Hermès.

Two-piece suit by Henry à la Pensée. Not yet the bikini, but the platform soles are there already.

on the list of conquered territories. Nearly all central European governments had fascist overtones, an orientation originally encouraged by the Western countries, which were keen to create a belt of resistance between communist Russia and themselves.

Germany mobilised. Terrified Jews were now trying to escape from officially organised pogroms, but it was difficult to leave Germany. Millions – impecunious, incredulous or religiously fatalistic – remained to await their fate. Italy, under pressure from Hitler, also passed anti-semitic laws, but never put them into practice. Jean Renoir's film *La Grande Illusion*,

the story of two French soldiers escaped from a POW camp during the last war, was oddly up to date, especially as one of them was Jewish. The war was still raging in Spain. Despite tremendous displays of courage, the Republicans, ill-equipped and badly organised, were losing ground. Franco's troops, not yet in Madrid, launched an offensive in Catalonia. Hundreds of destitute refugees crossed the Pyrenees in miserable convoys, ending up in French camps the other side of the border.

Life went on as usual despite the unwelcome and pessimistic warnings of a minority. Cocteau published his

mildly rebellious *Les Parents Terribles*. Sartre, later to be known as the father of Existentialism, published his novel *La Nausée*, thought to be depressing but talented. Sartre and his companion, the writer Simone de Beauvoir, had been among those who travelled to Spain, as sympathetic observers. Others included George Orwell, Jessica Mitford, André Malraux, Arthur Koestler, Ernest Hemingway (who published *To Have and Have Not* the previous year). For these and many others, the Spanish war had the tragic dimension of a modern crusade.

The Russians were waiting in the wings, aware that Western governments

Neat little coat by Rochas with matching skirt.

Opposite: *A flourish of hats by Dunton, Erik, Mado – with a Balenciaga suit, Lanvin Easter fantasy and Agnès.*

were more suspicious of them than of fascism. The great director Eisenstein filmed his historical epic *Alexander Nevsky*, which exalted the national spirit of the Russian people fighting the Teutonic invader. Although the story was set in medieval times, the intended parallel was clear. Prokofiev's score added greatly to the effect of this masterly cinematic fresco.

On the other side of the Atlantic, Americans did not want to be bothered with Europeans, the wars and the threats of war. They had enough troubles of their own. Floods had followed the devastating drought. John Steinbeck's novels, particularly *The Grapes of Wrath*, depicted the plight of the small farmers. The automobile industry had been hard hit by strikes. Managements reacted brutally and were supported by the police. America had made vast strides in the industrial sphere despite the Depression, and anything that theatened material progress was

sacrilege. There were nineteen million cars in the USA, nine times more than in France or England. There were three million refrigerators compared to as few as 3000 in England. The American government decided to approve fixed hours and minimum wages and to prohibit child labour. These basic reforms were as far as it was willing to go and many manufacturers thought even this to be a sin against the gospel of self-help and free enterprise. Franklin D. Roosevelt had been re-elected to the presidency. He was a controversial figure, an intelligent, energetic and dynamic man. He needed all the drive he could muster to solve the country's economic, political and racial problems. Communists were a tiny and deeply unpopular minority, though a number of important intellectuals joined the party. They were defending the blacks at a time when lynchings were still common in certain states. The blacks themselves, still the most oppressed class, remained unorganised.

American women were certainly not going to let politics make them forget their looks – a woman's looks were part of her capital. But fashion reacted to uncertainty by taking a practical turn. Casual outfits were in; so were economy and the joys of country life. Platform cork soles for the beach were a striking novelty. Hats continued to be ingenious and amusing, with inventive combinations of shapes and textures. They were, so to speak, fighting their own battle, still compulsory in town but obviously superfluous for outdoor activities. Many young women began to discard a hat in favour of a scarf or were prepared to rely on a good perm to keep their hair in shape. They wore it tightly pinned up or else in waves on the shoulders, Hollywood style. Hollywood's influence also meant that uplifted bosoms and extrovert sex-appeal were fashionable.

1939

Marlene Dietrich on her last trip to Paris before the
war broke out. She already looks quite military.

The war was over in Spain, but it left a nasty scar that was not to heal easily. Artists were to write Republican Spain's epitaph – prisoners at dawn counting the steps of wardens in empty corridors, tinkling keys, men waiting for their names to be called out in daily expectation of death – exiles who for years were to argue the pros and cons of lost battles and dream of better tomorrows while Franco established his own order, soon recognised by France and England. France had finally started to rearm. So had America.

George VI realistically came to visit Roosevelt, and it was not difficult to guess why, as women and children were already being evacuated from London and trenches were dug in the parks, shelters prepared, bags of sand piled up against buildings and works of art carefully removed.

The Americans were not impressed. They did not want to know, or rather, as Lindbergh put it: "They knew where their borders were – and these were not in Europe. They had had to deal with a Europe dominated by France and England, they might now have to learn of a Europe dominated by Germany." The 22,000 Nazis who had met in Madison Square Garden in February must have been much encouraged. Anyway, even though regular flights were now operating between Europe and the USA, most Americans felt their country was too far away to fear anything. Roosevelt's defence plans met with strong opposition: "Vote for him and you will be offering gas masks for Christmas." There was also a strong anti-semitic campaign, and ugly posters could be seen on the walls. Britain could not pretend the danger was so distant. "Hang out the washing on the Siegfried line", people sang to give themselves some heart. A war was to come, just as the four millionth house, the last one of a building programme started in 1918, had been

finished. What a shame, what a waste it would be.

In Paris, the season had got under way with the restraints imposed by uncertainty. Some artists, such as Edith Piaf and Tino Rossi, were still performing in Germany. Members of high society were making their own plans. Emigration to the USA was one solution for those who were most at risk but many did not consider leaving at all. They preferred to think that life

would continue in much the same way, war or no war.

There were some good films: John Ford's *Stagecoach*, Jean Renoir's *La Règle du Jeu* – its topical theme was human confusion when the time comes to make vital decisions – and Cukor's *The Women*, with Joan Crawford. She painted her lips a butterfly or bow-tie shape that was soon widely copied. But Germany invaded Czechoslovakia, then she invaded Poland – and that

was as much as the Allies could
tolerate: in September, Great Britain
and France declared war on Germany.
Meanwhile, there was the shock of the
Germano-Russian pact. Russia had
been left free to invade Poland and
later Finland, in the pursuit of
ambitions that went back to the days of
the Czars. Of course, France was not
ready for war at all, far less so indeed
than the British. A contingent of
158,000 British soldiers landed in
France. It was strange to see the
flat-helmeted Tommies marching
through the northern towns again,
though nothing had yet happened. The
whole thing was unreal, bewildering,
but all the same, people who had
somewhere to go started packing up,
carefully closing shutters. They locked
their doors and boarded trains for the
south.

Nobody quite knew what to expect
but *Vogue* continued to lay down rules
of conduct. It had spotted some
open-toed shoes in town and was not
having it. No *laissez aller*, please. It
was no good invoking circumstances –
women could have a war to face but
they must dress for dinner. In
London, Digby Morton was
advertising the 'siren suit', an outfit
surely elegant enough for those who
had to rush down the shelters in the
blackout. In Paris, fashionable life
came to a standstill, despite *Vogue*.
Chanel, Schiaparelli and many others
closed down. Those who had reliable
sources of information knew more than
the masses about the enormous
military might of the Germans. They
began to be frightened. And they
could afford a mobility denied to the
man in the street.

For the American public, the most
captivating drama of all was one which
was unrolled on the screen. *Gone with
the Wind* had at last been released.
The New York Film Critics' Circle had
preferred to vote *Wuthering Heights*
the best Hollywood film of the year
because they disapproved of the

Suit by Balenciaga with contrasting panels. This fashion best suited elegant women. Hat by Bruyère.

Drum hat by Charlotte. The other by Schiaparelli.

anti-democratic and anti-Negro aspects of its rival. But the film was a tremendous and lasting popular success. *Gone with the Wind* had all the ingredients of a smash-hit: a glamorous couple – the manly Clark Gable and pretty green-eyed Vivien Leigh (she was the wife of Laurence Olivier and had been until then a relatively obscure actress); plus the romance of the old South, its crinolines and classical white mansions, the glamour of uniforms and the agonies of a fratricide struggle. Thousands of women would have given anything to live through a war like that!

1940~43

Paquin. During the war, evening dresses often looked as if they were designed for romantic films.

The German onslaught, when it came, was irresistible. Norway, Denmark, Holland, Luxemburg, Belgium – they all fell. Some European royal families took refuge in England, as did all those who were determined to escape German occupation. Food was now rationed in England and the nation was prepared for the worst. Churchill had spelt it out in his "blood, sweat, toil and tears" speech. The French fled, blocking the roads to the south, machine-gunned by the German air force. A wealthy minority remained. Some, like Cocteau, Chanel and Schiaparelli, took over the Ritz Hotel, where a semblance of the old life could be preserved, but they soon left. Molyneux retreated to London, Schiaparelli and Mainbocher to New York. They left just in time, as the British army was cornered at Dunkirk and was trying desperately to recross the Channel. But on the Côte d'Azur and in Biarritz, social life kept going. Madame Pétain, mild and bosomy, was staying at Hendaye with her budgerigars until the Germans took over the hotel. Her elderly husband, a faded hero of the last war, made believe he was leading a national government, now based in Vichy. The Germans entered Paris in June – an old dream come true. They found the city fascinating, even deserted and dead as it temporarily was. Physically, it did not suffer greatly.

The Germans now concentrated their assault upon England. There was heavy bombing of civilian targets. There was the Battle of Britain and the London Blitz, the uncontrollable fires, the dead bodies among the dust and rubble. Many other cities had suffered or were to suffer the same. More than 4000 people had been killed by November. In turn, the RAF started night bombings over Germany. The USA helped Great Britain – thanks to the re-election of Roosevelt, the American arms factories were in full production. Convoys crossed the

Atlantic under constant attack from the dreaded German U-boats. In 1940 alone, 160,000 tons of shipping were sunk.

Then, in 1941, Germany invaded Russia, taking Stalin by surprise. The Japanese, now allied to the Germans, opened the war in the Far East from China to Indo-China. America was stunned by the news of the Japanese raid on their fleet at Pearl Harbour. Disastrous as it was, the attack on

Pearl Harbour at least gave Roosevelt the cause he needed to openly involve America. He declared war on Japan and subsequently on both Germany and Italy. War was escalating all over the world at a scale never known before.

The Germans met their first major defeat in North Africa: General Rommel was forced to retreat. Meanwhile, the Russians stopped the invasion of their country at the very

109

A good example of wartime dress: padded shoulders, effect of corselet and floral pattern. Germaine Lecomte.

By Orcel, Albouy and Ejad. Such photos had to bear the German censor's stamp before publication.

gates of Moscow and Leningrad. Everywhere, civilians endured extreme suffering. Jews were packed in cattle trains and moved towards torture and death in extermination camps. Many were gassed on arrival and were reduced to ashes in the camps' ovens. Wherever resistance occurred in Europe, it was efficiently persecuted by the SS. But nevertheless, people did continue to resist. Life had to go on.

Everything was rationed. In England, utility clothes came in and models were photographed on location in factories or beside bomb craters. The clothes they wore did not have much to offer that had not been seen in previous peacetime years. It was all a matter of transforming, altering, of making do with poor quality materials. Make-up disappeared from the shops. So too did stockings, so socks became chic. French milliners made hats they called

After the cars had disappeared. Perm,
practical shoulder bag, floral print and
platform shoes.

'bibis' – two feathers on top of a bit of straw and a little piece of net. *Haute couture* had not entirely disappeared, although the Germans at first wanted to move it to Berlin or Vienna. Lelong, representing the couturiers, bargained hard and obtained much: exemption from restrictions for twelve fashion houses – but ninety-two still managed to function. Eventually, no less than sixty survived, even cooperating with one another. Four models instead of fifteen would show thirty outfits instead of the usual hundred. There were still customers, not only the Germans but also anyone who had managed to maintain the old standards or who, through profitable black marketing, had acquired a quick fortune.

In 1942, the war was at its gloomiest. The Japanese were rapidly invading South-East Asia. Bombings intensified. The first landing raid, at Dieppe, was a failure and left more than 3500 Canadian dead on the beaches. American bombers raided France daily, the Germans took over the unoccupied zone and the siege of Stalingrad began.

Then, hope returned. In 1943, the American General Eisenhower landed in North Africa and von Paulus surrendered to the Russians at Stalingrad after months of house-to-house fighting in inhuman conditions. The Germans were driven out of Tunisia and Allied troops landed in Sicily. Soon, Italy surrendered as well. The toll was now so heavy that Germany had to conscript women and young boys.

The arts survived, but most creative work had to await the time when the world would have leisure for more than mere survival.

1944~45

*The last collection of the war at Fath's. Piled-up hair, turbans, sensible shoes.
The model looks as unsophisticated as the dress she is presenting.*

The first 'free' collection in the same premises. The journalist wears a war correspondent's badge.

The advantage now lay with the Allied armies and German defeat was not far away. The siege of Monte Cassino, in Italy, cost many lives. Germany was losing on all fronts and was also continually bombed. So was London, but two days after the Fifth Army entered Rome, an armada emerged from the mists of dawn in sight of the beaches of Normandy: the D-Day landings had begun – men in their thousands tumbled on to the sand, braving the heavy fire from bunkers hidden in the cliffs. The massive offensive was more than the Germans could sustain. The road to Paris would soon be open. Paris itself rose in insurrection and was ready to receive the Allied armies in triumph: Americans, British, Canadians, and the men of all nationalities who had chosen to fight under their flags. First to arrive was General Leclerc. De Gaulle made his entry late in August. The summer was hot and sunny. Feverish crowds gathered, filling the streets, chasing the last German troopers, dragging along those women who were known to have enjoyed the occupiers' favours. Barefooted, with their heads shaved, they were the humiliated scapegoats of a populace that had so often been submitted to humiliation.
Liberation in France had many cross-currents. There were the genuine members of the Resistance and the last-minute turncoats. There were the brave, the profiteers, the *miliciens* who had worked against their own people. The majority, however, were simply immensely relieved. They had waited in hope for this day, anxiously listening to BBC broadcasts and trying to make out puzzling messages such as: "The bearded man is rolling at the horizon. I repeat, three times: the bearded man is rolling at the horizon." Only members of the Resistance could interpret these as warnings of clandestine landings, of pin-point bombings, or of invasion.

The Americans had not yet overcome the Japanese, and there were massive air raids on Tokyo. Roosevelt had been re-elected for a fourth term. Scientific research had led to the development of the lethal V1 and V2 rockets – the last fell on England in 1945 – while the USA now possessed the atomic bomb. On 12 April 1945, Roosevelt died. On the 28th, Mussolini ended his life on a butcher's hook and on the 30th Hitler, in the depths of his Berlin bunker,

committed suicide with his wife Eva Braun. So too did Goebbels, his wife and their six children. Above them, Berlin, now a pile of charred rubble, was falling into the hands of the Russian troops. Germany had no choice but surrender. Japan, by her continual resistance, gave the Americans a pretext to try their new weapon: the country capitulated five days after Nagasaki and Hiroshima were disintegrated by atomic bombs.

This is the first professional picture of the young Bettina, who was to become a top model.

The world had now to lick its wounds and start anew. Refugees, displaced persons, camp survivors in their thousands and demobilised soldiers, were trying to return to what had been a home and was now often a pile of debris from which remnants of families had fled to uncertain destinations and fates. In all, many more than thirty million people had perished. Many more had been maimed physically and morally.

The war in China had been a three-cornered struggle between Chiang Kai-shek, the Japanese and the communists. Mao was ready to break his temporary alliance with the Kuomintang and was more than ever determined to free his country from foreign interference and Japanese occupation. In no country did the end of the war bring instant prosperity. Food, textiles and many other commodities remained scarce and rationed. So much had to be rebuilt. Yet in Paris *haute couture* was not only surviving but was planning the future. Jacques Fath, who had begun to design shortly before the war, now opened his own house, followed in 1945 by Pierre Balmain, who had been trained by Molyneux and Lelong. Fashion was not ready for innovation. It remained much the same as it had been in the war years, but new ideas were beginning to take root. After four years of isolation and stagnation, Paris was rediscovering an America that had freely evolved. Europe and the USA had to renew their links. On both sides of the Atlantic there was much to be seen, read and learned.

From the USA came plays like O'Neill's *Long Day's Journey into Night* and Tennessee Williams' *The Glass Menagerie*, books like Hemingway's *For Whom the Bell Tolls*, Scott Fitzgerald's *The Last Tycoon*, music like Gershwin's *Rhapsody in Blue*. Most popular of all were the new musicals, especially *Oklahoma*. Popular cinema magazines were

Fashion is still very static, as this dress by Lelong shows.

Worth in Paris again, with horizontal accordion sleeves. The picture was taken on 8th May, VE Day.

Tailored suit by Worth with pockets as a huge bow.

reproducing pictures of the Hollywood pin-ups: Virginia Mayo, Rosalind Russell and Lana Turner. New films arrived in great numbers – the back-log of Hollywood production during the war, among them Chaplin's *The Great Dictator*, an acid parody of Hitler which had been made in 1940, the same year as Disney's *Fantasia*. The exceptional Orson Welles had made *Citizen Kane*, a powerful film that took cinema techniques a giant step forward. Lubitsch's *To Be or Not To Be* starred Carole Lombard, who had married Clark Gable shortly before she was killed in an air crash; and *To Have and Have Not*, based on Hemingway's novel, was the first feature film in which Lauren Bacall played opposite Humphrey Bogart. All these entertainments Europe had missed, and to the young they came

with the force of a revolution. Frank Sinatra and other crooners were also a fascinating novelty, singing music of a kind unfamiliar to Europeans, but their popularity was greater in England than anywhere else in Europe. Graham Greene had written *The Power and the Glory*, T. S. Eliot his *Four Quartets*, Noël Coward *Blithe Spirit*, Bertholt Brecht *Mother Courage*. The contrast between them could hardly have been greater. The leading literary figures in France were now Camus, the poets Eluard, Aragon and Sartre, who emerged as the most influential philosopher of the period with *L'Etre et le Néant*.
In European cinema, there were films like *How Green was my Valley*, Laurence Olivier's *Henry V*, Carné's *Les Visiteurs du Soir*, but the immediate post-war renaissance came from Italy, where a new generation of

directors, matured by their recent experiences, turned a sympathetic eye on ordinary people and the dramas of daily life. The first masterpiece of this school was Rossellini's *Rome, Open City*, with Anna Magnani, filmed mainly on location and deliberately realistic. It was to influence a whole generation of European directors. 1945 marked the end of a tragic era. Europe could now look forward to happier times.

1946~47

Dior's new line: full long skirt, tiny waist. The cuffs are tied in a bow.

Another Dior evening dress worn by Sylvie, a top model of charming simplicity.

Peace was a year old. In a Paris which was physically undamaged, a taste for the better things of life could again be indulged. The French were never reconciled to food rationing and this soon disappeared. Despite shortages, women were following the fashion for fuller and longer skirts as best they could. The waist was accentuated by a small corset. Probably thanks to American influence, the medium-sized French woman now had to look slimmer and taller. There was a return to sophistication and a departure from the natural look enforced by the war. Heels became higher. Tailored suits ingeniously made from discarded men's suits were a thing of the past. The fashion world took its lead from Paris once more.

But England, with a deficit of over a billion pounds, was imposing tighter restrictions than ever. The French were a subject of resigned envy. Television programmes returned, but they were only seen, however, by a mere 12,000 households. Museums had reopened and concerts were numerous, but people really preferred to forget their daily miseries in the darkness of the cinema. About twenty million people went to a film every week.

The British government introduced the National Health scheme and set about reconstructing the country amid grim shortages. In fact, neither British nor American governments were very happy with French frivolity. The fashion houses had to withdraw some of their more extravagant designs and make sober versions specially for export.

The place to be in Paris was St Germain des Prés. Sartre's theories on existentialism became a cult with young people for whom the war had meant the loss of four important years. The youthful existentialists started to meet in cellars in order to dance till dawn to the sounds of jazz or blues, or to listen to the disenchanted songs of Juliette

Long fur-trimmed jacket by Fath. The shoulders are still heavily padded.

Balenciaga kept to his own style.

Dress by Fath that imitates a coat. Bettina has lost her country girl looks and gained in sophistication.

Greco. The pathetic songs of the waif-like Edith Piaf were even more popular. Meanwhile, the Italians continued to produce earthy films. De Sica made *Shoeshine* and Rossellini *Paisa*.

Democracy was the reward many people wanted from the war. It was the needs of the majority which were now paramount. The cultural changes were too fundamental to be reversed – or were they?

Haute couture at least did not agree. It was trying to regain its wealthy clientele and put the clock back.

A new couturier, mainly trained by Lelong, as was Balmain, opened his doors in 1947. He was backed by Marcel Boussac, a textile manufacturer. Within weeks, the shy Christian Dior

was being talked of everywhere. Magic, sensational, beautiful, Dior's creations literally saved the prestige of French fashion, a genius who eclipsed the talents of the others. Dior changed the whole feminine image responding to every woman's secret aspiration. "I design clothes for flower-like women, with round shoulders, full, feminine bust and hand-span waists above enormous spreading skirts." It was the right antidote to years of monotonous austerity and privations. A Dior dress took from fifteen to eighty yards of fabric, and there were equally voluminous flounced petticoats underneath. Absolute folly, and more than both the indignant American and British governments were prepared to tolerate. Conscious of the enthusiasm

this new fashion had provoked, they reacted with official protests. The buyers ignored them. One London store sold 700 Dior copies within two weeks. Dior showed his collection at Neimann-Marcus in the USA. Less publicised was the secret show he put on at the French Embassy in London for the Queen, Princess Margaret and the Duchess of Kent.

1948~49

Winter dress by Fath with zip at the
cuffs, fur bow and ingenious sun-ray
pleated panel.

Velvet evening dress lined with satin by
Balmain. The under bodice emerges in a
bow from the corselet.

*Evening dress by Fath, made of heavy
satin with pearl embroidery and worn by
Sophie, a model of great chic who later
married Anatole Litvak.*

The world was like a huge jigsaw
puzzle, but the war had scattered the
pieces in great disorder and some of
them were even missing. So it had to
be partly redesigned – nations had to
find stability – economic, political and
cultural; conflicting aspirations had to
be satisfied – preferably peacefully.
Yet, hardly a year after India had
achieved independence amid
unprecedented bloodshed, the
non-violent Gandhi was assassinated.
Stalin still had some personal accounts
to settle and his country, despite the
loss of twenty million people during
the war, had become disquietingly
powerful. It was obvious that Stalin
wished to enlarge Russia's sphere of
influence and, after obtaining part of
Germany – leaving half of Berlin
isolated in the middle – he had
designs on other Eastern European
countries. Also, Russia had carried out
its first atomic tests in 1949 and this
was felt by the Americans to be a direct
threat. The fact that they themselves
had been the first to unleash the atom
only increased their anxiety.
Deeply suspicious of Russian
intentions, the Americans reacted by
stiffening their diplomatic line and at
home started a purge of all known
communists. This witch hunt was
later to take hysterical proportions. It
reached the point where internment
camps were secretly prepared, though
never used.
China had completed its swing to the
left. Chiang Kai-shek fled to Taiwan
while the victorious Mao Tse-tung and
his Premier Chou En-lai proclaimed
the first Communist People's Republic.
In the Middle East, the new state of
Israel was born after a violent struggle
with the British and with the profound
disapproval of the Arab world. The
murder of six million Jews during the
war and the failure of the European
powers to prevent this crime weighed
on the consciences of Western
statesmen and led them to support the
establishment of a Jewish state.

Winter collection at Balmain's. The girls are now taller and slim following the American standards of beauty.

Winter outfit with large fur-trimmed stole. Jacqueline Auriol, a jet pilot, sits in the background, in a white skirt.

Europe was hastily, and often carelessly, rebuilding its cities. There was too little money and there were too many homeless. Consequently, instead of designing an environment which would create a sense of community, architects and civil servants alike opted for uninspired blocks of flats planted haphazardly on sites where their ugliness disfigured the townscape. Here, people were unable to communicate with each other and children relied on vandalism to quench their boredom. Up went the slums of the future. High-rise flats offered the cheapest solution but it was in the long run to prove costly, as they were the breeding grounds of endless social problems.

In 1947, England fêted the wedding of Princess Elizabeth to Philip Mountbatten, later created Duke of Edinburgh. Prince Charles was born the following year. The British royal family naturally preferred British designs and shopped at home. Hardy Amies, who had opened in 1946, was one of its favourite couturiers, and Norman Hartnell another.

Meanwhile, Dior was enjoying a tremendous success and had completely conquered the world of fashion. His visit to New York in 1948 clearly underlined the importance of business links between the ready-to-wear industry and the prestigious fashion houses which private customers could no longer support. Ready-to-wear had developed tremendously over the years and the

survival of *haute couture* depended largely on its success with manufacturers: it was more realistic to deal with them than to cater for a diminished minority by opening branches abroad – in the certain knowledge that Paris models would be widely copied all the same. America was industrially advanced, the country had not suffered from destruction and prosperous Americans provided the necessary mass market.

Although poverty existed, the USA represented the land of plenty to impoverished Europeans and it had self-confidence to match. All Europeans remembered the impression of opulence made by the well-fed soldiers of an army that could afford to waste so much and think so little of it.

The cinema also conveyed this image of wealth. If Dassin's *Naked City* was an attempt to show American life in a way familiar from the films of the Italian realists, movies like *Gilda* or even Orson Welles' *The Lady of Shanghai* were all that many Europeans had at their disposal as a portrait of the USA.

Rita Hayworth, long, slim, beautiful and sexy, was the star of both these films. Together with the other Hollywood stars, she represented the American woman. It was a shock for Europeans to meet the ordinary Americans who travelled on the first package tours. The best fashion photographers, like the Americans Irving Penn and Norman Parkinson, preferred to maintain the illusion. They used slim sophisticated girls who met the American standards of beauty. They did not correspond to the way European women looked, but they did

enhance the elegance of any outfit. The couturiers created their designs for this new type while millions of women tried in vain to alter their own figures in order to match the new ideal.

Awareness of the body could only lead to a growing concern for sexual matters. Sexiness was the concern of film producers; sex had been the moving force in Freud's theories; and Dr Kinsey implanted it deep in the popular consciousness in 1948. American culture had become autonomous. Tennessee Williams' *A Street Car Named Desire*, Norman Mailer's *The Naked and the Dead* (published in 1948) and Arthur Miller's *Death of a Salesman*, produced in 1949, owed nothing to European influences. It was the turn of artists like Jackson Pollock to influence European painters.

In Europe, the Italian cinema still

continued to produce a number of good realistic films: De Santis made *Bitter Rice* in 1948 and De Sica *Bicycle Thieves* – both now classics. The French argued about Clouzot's strong *Quai des Orfèvres* and were fascinated by the talent of actors such as Jean-Louis Barrault and dancers such as Roland Petit. The latter had just founded Les Ballets de Paris and had successfully produced the ballet *Carmen* with his wife Zizi Jeanmaire in the principal part. She was a piquant young woman who managed to look boyishly feminine with a short straight haircut that was soon in fashion. It suited large-eyed elfin faces like that of Audrey Hepburn.

Simone de Beauvoir wrote *The Second Sex*, a book that can be considered the first feminist work of the post-war epoch. French women had only acquired the right to vote in 1945 and there was still much to be done about

A refined dress by Fath with built-in bolero.

Suit by Fath. The blouse has an unusual collar and the enormous pockets are very much part of the jacket.

women's lot. Their part in society had become increasingly important and the old patterns could no longer apply. Fashion, thanks mostly to Dior, was everyone's concern. Paper patterns saw to it that home-made outfits could be up to date and elegant. Dior had imposed the tiny waist and much longer skirts – either very full or very narrow. Coats were A-shaped, jackets could be short for tailored suits or flouncy, sleeves were bulky to accentuate the hour-glass effect or, by contrast, were slim. In fact, evening dresses were about the only garments to show any unity of shape: they were mostly strapless, with long full skirts which needed yards of material. Cocktail dresses were usually narrower and shorter but were hardly less splendid than the full-length evening dresses that in these years reached the heights of magnificence. Dior, Fath and Balmain's dresses in particular were fabulous, often with much embroidery and beading.

On the whole, designers were freely improvising on the basis of a very slim but shapely figure.

Fashion had never changed so quickly. It altered practically from one collection to another. Couturiers used sophisticated cuttings with great skill and obtained a wide variety of effects. This period was the renaissance of *haute couture* and gifted apprentices were ready to follow in their masters' steps.

Jacket by Paquin in melon slices with big $\frac{3}{4}$-length circular sleeves.

123

Another of Dior's huge pocketed
creations with a draped crossed-over top.

Draped tailored suit by Dior with padde[d]
raglan sleeves. Only for the very slim.

The world at last seemed to be taking shape. The Americans and the Russians were both trying to assert their supremacy in the world and this resulted in the Cold War. The most serious physical conflict erupted in Korea and soon the Chinese became involved. The Americans feared lest the whole Far East slip away from their influence. It would upset the world balance and this balance was the new political concept. Realpolitik was back in business. While Kurosawa was filming his beautiful *Rashomon*, the Japanese were still the prime villains of scores of Hollywood productions. America had not yet fully awakened from the Far Eastern wartime nightmare, even though American forces had occupied Japan. Thor Heyerdahl left on his *Kon Tiki* for the first of many explorations of its kind, and while Hindemith optimistically entitled his latest symphony *Harmony of the World*, Jerome Robbins and Leonard Bernstein more sceptically produced a ballet called *Age of Anxiety*. Jean-Paul Sartre wrote *La Mort dans l'Ame*, and the Pope issued a decree against his existentialist theories, which must indeed have pleased their author. Malraux had returned to humanist pursuits and wrote his *Psychology of Art*.

Though the world was at peace, the middle-aged found it hard to forget their wartime apprehensions. For the young, on the other hand, life lacked purpose and excitement. They were growing up in a vacuum. Wilder filmed *Sunset Boulevard*, a homage to and an epitaph for the first age of cinema, the great era of dream and fantasy. In the film were two great survivors of this epoch, von Stroheim and Gloria Swanson, who had been the star of Stroheim's own silent features. The new film stars included Elizabeth Taylor, Burt Lancaster, Marlon Brando, James Dean and Marilyn Monroe. Everybody was whistling the compelling theme of Carol Reed's *The Third Man*, a film that could not have been much farther from Hollywood's frame of mind. Western Europeans were openly eager to enjoy material comfort on the American model.

Clothes were no longer rationed in England. In Paris, fashion remained firmly in the hands of Dior, Fath and Balenciaga, but this dominance was not to last: two young couturiers, Givenchy and Cardin, started in 1951 and 1952 respectively. In 1954, Chanel reopened: would she be successful again? Schiaparelli closed down and Fath died.

Dior's death in 1957 marked the end of an era that had been short but brilliant. The great tradition of *haute couture* continued, but the new generation was more casual and oriented towards people of their own age group, who had always been rather neglected by their elders. The fashion revolution was to explode, unexpectedly, in England. In 1955, Mary Quant modestly started a small shop – not a *salon* – in Chelsea – not Mayfair. The new fashion did not emerge from London quite by chance: the British were more directly influenced by the American way of life, where the accent was on youth. Besides, the French were too traditional: their society people were not likely to stand aside so that the young could fulfil their fantasies. But they could not resist for long. Fashion had ceased to be the privilege of a leading minority. Would it be able to influence an independent new wave? What would fashion mean to the jeans generation?